the *How to Identify* series

How to Identify

ENGLISH SILVER

DRINKING VESSELS

600 - 1830

THE *How to Identify* SERIES

How to Identify English Drinking Glasses and Decanters, 1680–1830
by Douglas Ash

How to Identify Persian Rugs and other Oriental Rugs
by C. Delabère May

How to Identify Antique Maps, Charts and Globes
by Raymond Lister
(*for publication in 1964*)

How to Identify
ENGLISH SILVER DRINKING VESSELS 600-1830

by

DOUGLAS ASH

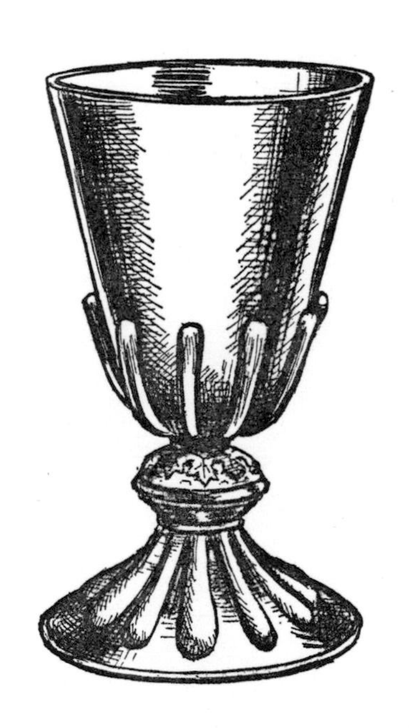

G. BELL AND SONS LTD
LONDON

York House, Portugal Street
London, W.C.2

Printed in Great Britain by
The Camelot Press Ltd., London and Southampton

Acknowledgments

THE AUTHOR wishes to acknowledge his indebtedness to Christ's College, Cambridge, The Historic Churches Preservation Trust, The Worshipful Company of Goldsmiths, The Victoria and Albert Museum, The British Museum, the Vicar of Cirencester, Mr. J. F. Hayward, and Mr. Arthur Grimwade, F.S.A. He also wishes to express his thanks to Lady Lovering Phillips, who kindly read the proofs.

CONTENTS

PHOTOGRAPHS

DRAWINGS

INTRODUCTION

IF IT was seldom the practice in England to serve butter in a lordly dish, at least it cannot be denied that wine or other liquor was very often served in a lordly drinking vessel. Drinking vessels form the most important single group of objects in the history of the craft of silversmithing, and it is therefore fitting that they should be dealt with in a book devoted exclusively to the subject.

This survey commences at the earliest date at which the English could be said to exist as a nation and from which examples still survive. It ends in the early 19th century because, thereafter, comparatively few silver drinking vessels were made, and design had begun to flounder in a sea of eclecticism and confused experiment.

The division of a subject such as this into fixed periods is always bound to be more or less invalid, because there was always a great deal of overlapping, and styles often continued to appear long after they had ceased to be truly fashionable. But the periods represented by the various chapters have been selected as being more readily comprehensible to the reader, and furthermore, there was always an epoch to which any given style more properly belonged than any other; it is this aspect of the matter which has been emphasized.

It will be noticed that the first chapter begins with the early Saxon era and ends with the late Middle Ages, covering a span of no less than nine hundred years, and this appears at first sight so disproportionate a period for one chapter, that some explanation must be given.

The fact is that surviving silver vessels dating from before 1500 are, as might be expected, far from plentiful. The Saxon period is represented by only a minute number of examples, and Norman specimens, apart from ecclesiastical plate, are almost non-existent or unrecognized. Even though mediaeval vessels are, in fact, available from time to time, it would be idle to pretend that they are easy to acquire. They are both rare and costly, and although there is always a chance that an early piece might be encountered by accident, it would be pointless, in a practical book concerned primarily with identification, to deal exhaustively with ancient artefacts which are seldom to be seen outside important museums, and are virtually uncollectable by any but the very wealthy or very fortunate.

Nevertheless, since this book is intended not only for the actual or potential collector, but also for those who are simply attracted to the subject by its inherent interest, and would wish to have their powers of appreciation enhanced by knowledge, it is desirable that no period should be wholly neglected if it has anything to show for itself by way of examples. Accordingly, although the earlier centuries may be but sparsely represented, they must be regarded as an essential part of the history of the subject.

It is only comparatively recently that silver objects have begun to be reverenced on account of their antiquity. To the peoples of past ages they were largely, apart from their beauty and utility, usable, durable investments, or a means of keeping a reserve of capital in a convenient form which would also enhance the prestige of the owners. If circumstances rendered such a course necessary or desirable, they were ruthlessly melted down and converted into money.

Heavy casualties also occurred as a result of changes in fashion, particularly at the close of the mediaeval period, and pieces which did not accord with prevailing design were frequently melted and rewrought, so that their antiquity may be regarded as the very cause of their destruction.

In view of these factors, it must be considered as something of a fortunate accident that any have survived at all in their original form, though it is amusing to reflect that some old silver vessels still in existence may embody the ghosts, as it were, of several rewrought ancestors dating back to the remotest antiquity.

In addition to drinking vessels which were entirely of silver, there were many others made of non-metallic substances mounted in silver or silver-gilt, and it would be impossible to present a complete picture without considering these also.

Various materials were employed, the most popular being horn, wood, marble, coco-nuts, ostrich eggs, hardstones, pottery and porcelain, the beautiful workmanship of the mounts sometimes appearing strangely at variance with the humble nature of the substance used for the body of the vessel. Some had a very long history, others waxed and waned according to the vagaries of fashion. They will all be discussed in the appropriate places.

The amateur of English silver enjoys an advantage which is denied to those whose interests lie in other branches of art history. This consists of a tidy and logical system of hall-marking which developed gradually over the years, and recorded an increasing amount of information. Students of furniture, painting, armour, glass, etc., are obliged to base their attributions and dating mainly on style, but a marked silver object made since the late Middle Ages often bears a permanent record of its maker, its quality, and its date and place of assay. Assaying is the official testing of silver to ensure that it approximates to, or exceeds, the legal standard of purity. Wares were submitted to this process soon after they were made, or even before they were entirely finished, so that the date of assay and the date of manufacture may generally be considered as more or less coincident.

Little is known of the organization of the craft, if any, before the year 1180, when the London goldsmiths, one of whom was a City alderman, were fined by King Henry II for forming a guild without royal consent, but it is probable that some kind of association had already existed for many years. Subsequent legislation affecting the goldsmiths—a term which comprehends silversmiths also—brought about certain progressive changes in hall-marking which will be discussed as they arise according to period, but it is quite clear that the framers of the various Acts had in mind, not the provision of evidence for the convenience of posterity, but the protection of the buying public against fraud.

It is hardly surprising that, in a trade concerned with articles made of precious metal, persons should have attempted from time to time to enrich themselves by dishonest means at the expense of the laity. The hall-marking laws made the public sale of objects made of base metal difficult and dangerous, and the marking of an obviously low-standard piece required the co-operation of responsible officials which was forthcoming, fortunately, on only a few isolated occasions, but other frauds were sometimes practised, such as the transposition of marks from genuine articles of modest value and true quality to low-grade, or spurious but apparently authentic ones of greater value.

The danger here probably stems no less from unscrupulous contemporary makers than from later traffickers in antique plate, and although it would be unreasonable to regard all old silver with suspicion, especially when offered by a reputable dealer, it is obviously desirable that the collector or student should exercise a general caution.

The chief safeguard against being deceived in the manner referred to is to learn, as far as possible, to identify the silver vessels of various periods on stylistic grounds, and to look to hall-marks only for final confirmation of one's judgment. No well-informed student would, for example, be beguiled by a late 18th-century goblet bearing a set of hall-marks cut from a spoon of the mid-17th century: apart from other factors he would know that such an object could not possibly have existed at the time suggested by the marks.

Apart from any question of fraud, a slavish attachment to hall-marks results in the exclusion of a great deal of highly interesting and artistically meritorious plate, which, never having been submitted for assay, bears only a maker's mark or no marks whatever. Although such vessels represent a technical infringement of the law, the quality of the metal generally approximates to the legal standard, and the intentions of the makers appear to have been mostly quite innocent. It is probable that the majority consists of pieces which were privately commissioned and not exposed for general sale, or replacements of unserviceable or unfashionable vessels made largely or wholly from the original metal.

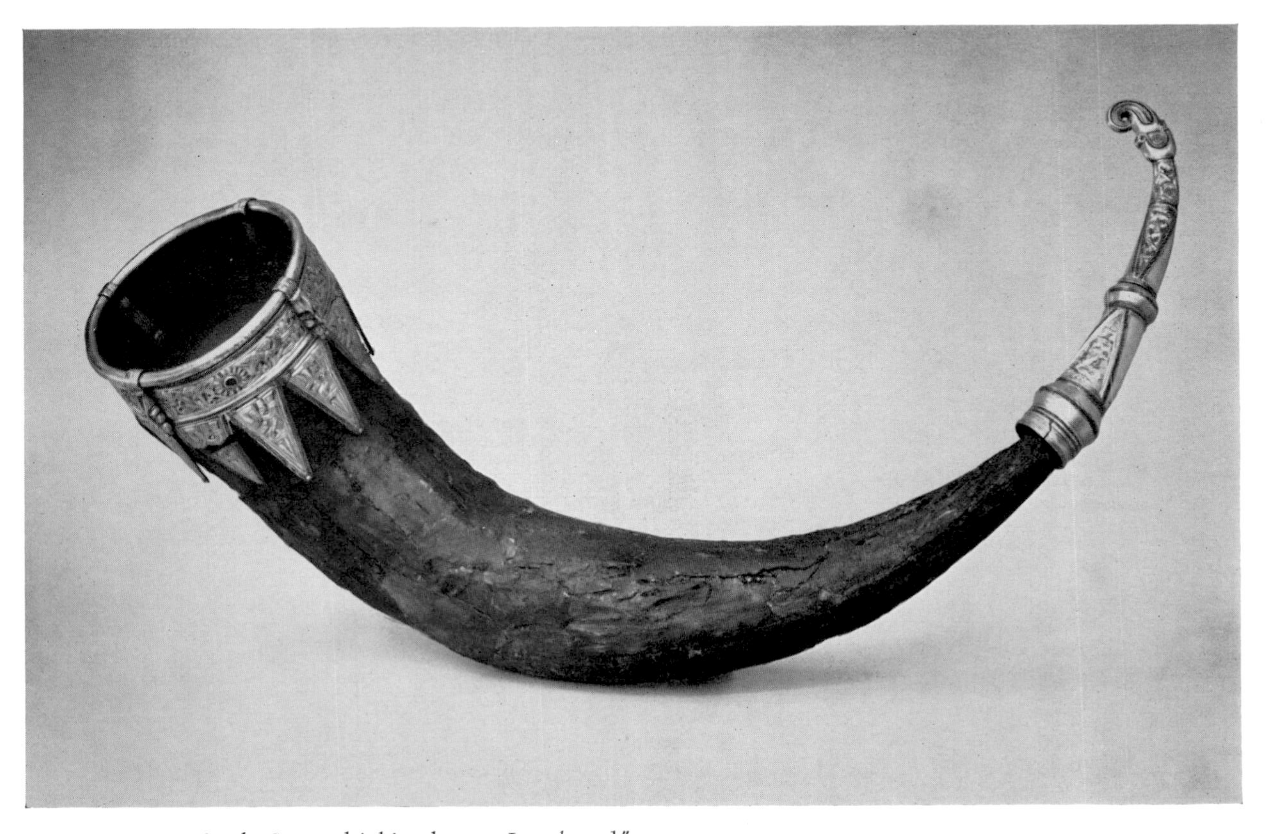

1. Anglo-Saxon drinking horn. *Length:* 19½″

(*British Museum*)

2a. Anglo-Saxon drinking bowl. *Height:* $3\frac{7}{10}''$

(*British Museum*)

2b. Anglo-Saxon standing cup. *Height:* $5\frac{1}{2}''$ (*British Museum*)

Much of this unmarked, or incompletely marked, plate is of magnificent technical and aesthetic quality, and as it is generally less expensive than marked specimens of the same kind, it makes a rare prize for the experienced student who has taken the trouble to study means of identification.

No attempt has been made in this book to provide lists of hall-marks, as to do so would be merely to duplicate the work of other writers who have dealt adequately with the same subject. Works of this kind are mentioned in the bibliography.

This book does not pretend to be an exhaustive survey of the very large subject under consideration; that would need several volumes. It sets out, by means of an analytical approach, to stimulate in the student an awareness of significant details both of form and decoration, from which the period of any given object may be broadly deduced by analogy. But the matter does not end there, and if the reader may be encouraged to pause, in the midst of his cold and logical diagnoses, to accept the creative message of the artist-craftsmen of past ages and rejoice in the beauty of the lovely medium in which they worked, the author will be well content.

CHAPTER ONE

THE SAXON AND MEDIAEVAL PRELUDE

600–1500

THE SAXON PERIOD

THE SAXON era, from the late 6th century to the 11th century, must be treated as a whole in the context of this book, because throughout this period there were probably no significant changes in the forms of drinking vessels, and the paucity of material makes it unprofitable to consider changes in decoration.

Anglo-Saxon beverages, apart from water, which does not seem to have been much in demand, consisted of ale, brewed from malted barley, wine, imported from western Europe where viticulture had been established by the Romans in the 3rd century, and mead, brewed from honey and malt. There were also compounds, such as pigment, comprising wine, honey, and spice, and morat, which was a mixture of honey and mulberry juice. Of all these the most popular were ale and mead, and the most popular vessel to contain them was the drinking horn.

DRINKING HORNS

These horns, of romantically barbaric appearance, varied very much in capacity; some were quite small, others were immense, holding up to a gallon and a half of liquor. They come within the sphere of this book because they were very often rimmed with silver, and sometimes tipped as well. An example preserved in the British Museum is shown in Plate 1. They are not plentiful, because partial survival in every case has probably depended on their having been buried, and this has generally caused the decomposition of the horn itself, although the silver mounts have remained largely unaffected.

The mounts of more than six were unearthed at Sutton Hoo in 1939, but the horns which they once embellished had mouldered away to nothing. These mounts, the fairly complete specimen in Plate 1, and certain pictorial evidence like that furnished by contemporary manuscripts show that there was no way of standing horns on a flat surface so that the contents remained unspilt; they had to be retained in the hand until they were empty (Fig. 1). In a bibulous age when even the clergy were

Fig. 1. Drinking horn in use

often drunk this was perhaps not considered any great hardship, but it will be seen that, later on, when becoming intoxicated had ceased to be almost the only form of recreation, steps were taken by silversmiths to remedy the inconvenience, but only after the horn had declined in popularity.

DRINKING BOWLS

Festive scenes in manuscripts and the Bayeux Tapestry depict, not only the horn, but also the drinking bowl, which usually rested in the hand of the drinker between the thumb and fingers, like a bird's nest in the fork of a tree. Contemporary sources of this kind naturally provide no clue as to the material from which the bowls were made; they may have been in wood, pottery, or base metal, but some, possibly more than we suspect, were quite certainly made wholly or partly of silver.

Several of these silver bowls, with and without covers, have survived, and the fact that the national origin of nearly every one of them is a matter of dispute among experts is of no great importance, as it merely indicates what one would have expected in any case—namely, that Anglo-Saxon styles showed an affinity with those of northern Europe in general. A British Museum example may be seen in Plate 2a, and Mr. Charles Oman[1] illustrates an almost undoubtedly English specimen of the same shape which is in the Copenhagen Museum.

Plain silver, depending for its effect on form alone, seems, with few exceptions, not to have recommended itself to the Anglo-Saxons any more than the Celts. They used various decorative techniques including embossing, engraving, and carving, the effect of the last being often heightened with niello, which consisted of an amalgam of silver, lead, copper, and sulphur. This was applied, in much the same way as enamel, in the lines and cavities forming the design in the surface of the object, and was then fused by heat. It was finally ground or filed level with the surrounding metal, and after polishing showed as a lustrous black against the whiteness of the silver. In 19th-century Russia, the technique was much used for snuff-boxes, and the hilts and scabbard-mounts of sabres and daggers, but has been out of favour in England for many centuries.

The actual designs covered a wide range within the limits of the prevailing artistic idiom, and included fishes, animals, grotesque masks, twining branches, or scrolls sometimes ending in crude monsters' heads, birds, and interlaced strapwork, displaying at times an almost Asiatic profusion.

Some of this ornament is shown in Fig. 2. A hoard of Celtic precious-metal objects, found in Orkney in the middle of the

[1] *English Domestic Silver*, 1947.

19th century, included coins of a 10th-century Abbasid Khalifah of Baghdad, and the fact is probably not without significance regarding the movement of artistic influences, possibly by means of the Swedish Vikings, who traded—and probably raided—

Fig. 2a. Saxon zoomorphic ornament

Fig. 2b. Saxon strapwork

Fig. 3. Saracenic strapwork

in the Black Sea and the eastern Mediterranean. The shape of many of the bowls was common among Islamic coppersmiths, and it is interesting to compare the example of Saxon strapwork in Fig. 2b with its Saracenic counterpart in Fig. 3.

BEAKERS

Contemporary manuscripts bear witness to the existence of beakers in Saxon England, and although their substance cannot be deduced from such sources, some of them were almost certainly made of precious metal. There are unfortunately no surviving examples in silver, at least above the surface of the ground, but it is necessary to afford them brief mention, because they remained popular throughout the greater part of the period covered by this book.

It is often assumed that the first beaker consisted of a natural cylinder of horn with a disc of horn fixed into the smaller end to form a base, but even if this is so, it must have been invented long before the Saxon invasions, for the Romans were making them in glass as early as the 1st century, and many were imported, before the conquest of Britain was complete, from the glass-making region between the Seine and the Rhine.

All beakers were of essentially the same shape, having straight or concave sides, and a flat base which was usually narrower than the mouth (Fig. 4). Actual examples in silver will have to be considered later.

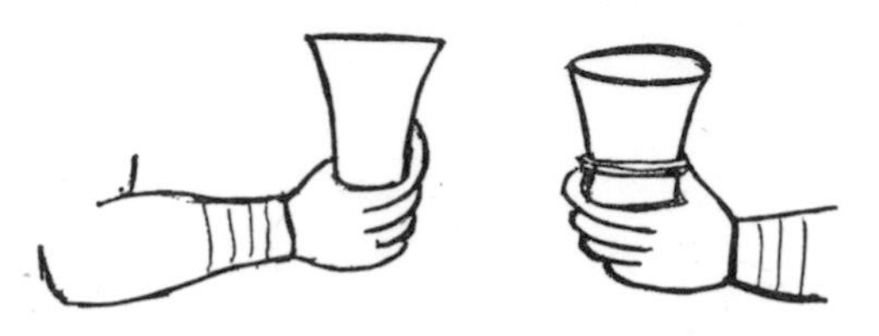

Fig. 4. Saxon beakers

STANDING CUPS

A standing cup consists of some kind of bowl or beaker, not standing upon its own proper base, but supported on a stem and foot. We shall probably never know to what extent such vessels were used for secular purposes in Saxon times, because the enormous quantities of plate looted by the Normans in 1066 must have left the country almost entirely denuded and, as little warning was received of the impending attack, no one could have had much time to bury anything.

Repeated Viking incursions, however, had left the earlier inhabitants of coastal areas and estuaries in some degree prepared for further attacks by the same enemies, and in the late 18th century a silver standing cup, buried in about 875, but possibly very considerably older, was excavated in Cornwall where it may have been hidden to preserve it from raiding Vikings. This cup, illustrated in Plate 2b, may be seen in the British Museum.

Its original purpose is not quite certain, though one of the other objects found with it suggests that it may have been a chalice, but the assumption which is often made that such drinking vessels were made exclusively for liturgical purposes is unwarrantable, for although the early Church was the most important patron of the goldsmiths, secular cups of the same basic type, in various materials, were well known in Roman Britain, and their use as drinking vessels in Saxon England is well attested by manuscript illustrations.

Fig. 5. Saxon standing cup

Fig. 6. Saxon standing cups

Fig. 5, from an 11th-century manuscript, shows a servant offering a standing cup, and Fig. 6 from the same source illustrates two others standing on a table. While it is possible that some of these cup-like objects were, in fact, containers for salt, it seems likely, in view of the habits of our Saxon ancestors, that most of them were drinking vessels.

Another manuscript of the same period also depicts a festive board, part of which may be seen in Fig. 7. In spite of the curious

Fig. 7. 11th-century standing cup

perspective it is of some importance, as it shows, *inter alia*, a secular standing cup of a form which is often considered as having first appeared in the 12th century.

English silver of the period must have enjoyed a certain prestige. A Saxon king took silver vessels with him as presents when he visited Rome in the middle of the 9th century, and an Anglo-Saxon school of goldsmiths, working for the Holy See, was already established there. These facts may help us to understand the admiration of the Norman chronicler, William of Poitiers, when he wrote: 'Men gazed in wonder on the rich spoils of the conquered island,' and 'the vessels of silver or gold were marvelled at.'

THE NORMAN PERIOD

Silver drinking vessels of the Norman period, that is to say, the period when the Norman style of architecture was prevalent, are so excessively rare that there is little to be said about them. There seems no doubt that beakers, bowls, and standing cups continued to be used, though it is unlikely that drinking horns remained as popular as in pre-conquest days, but the only class represented by an actual specimen is the standing cup.

Fig. 8. 12th-century standing cup

The example in question, of the type shown in Fig. 8, is a 12th-century chalice of low-grade silver, found in 1890 in the stone coffin of Archbishop Hubert Walter in Canterbury Cathedral. As ecclesiastical authorities were not given to squandering their more valued possessions, it may be assumed that this cup was old and of little account at the time of the archbishop's death in 1205. It is generally considered to date from about 1160.

The shape of the wide, shallow bowl is of some importance, because it remained almost the standard form until well into the 14th century. It should also be noted that the stem, if it can be said to exist at all, is a mere upward extension of the foot, terminating immediately below the knop, or 'knot', as it was called in the Middle Ages. The whole cup bears a striking resemblance to the 11th-century secular cup in Fig. 7.

A change in the profile of the lower part in the following century left the stem and foot more clearly distinguished from each other.

THE 13TH CENTURY

STANDING CUPS

Several examples of standing cups of the 13th century are still in existence, and are, without exception, ecclesiastical chalices, but there is strong evidence that many secular drinking vessels were of precisely the same form.

Plate 3a illustrates a parcel (partly) gilt chalice in the British Museum from the church of Berwick St. James, Wiltshire. It will be observed that the bowl is almost identical with that of the 12th-century example in Fig. 8, but the portion of the stem below the knop is quite clearly defined, and the slope of the foot is greatly diminished. This is, in fact, in all respects a typical plain chalice of the 13th century, and in many respects a typical drinking vessel.

Fig. 9, which is taken from a 13th-century memorial slab in

St. Bride's church, Glamorgan,[1] shows the arms of Sir John Butler. These consist of three standing cups with covers, and are a patent allusion to the owner's name. As it was the duty of a butler to keep his master provided with liquor, it is evident that cups of this kind, which are identical in form to the Berwick

Fig. 9. 13th-century standing cups in shield of arms

St. James chalice, were for secular use, and furthermore, chalices were never provided with permanent covers. In these circumstances, the chalice illustrated in Plate 3a will serve as an example of a secular, as well as an ecclesiastical vessel of the period, and it is quite possible that it came into the possession of the church as the gift, from a lay benefactor, of one of his domestic utensils.

COCO-NUT CUPS

It is in the middle years of the 13th century that we encounter the first reference to a Coco-nut cup, but as we can have no definite idea of the appearance of such a vessel at this period, there would be no point in considering the matter further.

It is evident from an ordinance of Henry III in 1238 that silversmithing activities in London were expanding to such an extent

[1] *Memorial Brasses and Slabs*, Charles Boutell, 1847.

that the authorities felt obliged to regulate them, and the ordinance made it compulsory for members of the craft to use metal of the same standard as the silver coinage.

THE 14TH CENTURY

Sir Charles Jackson listed, in his monumental work,[1] the names of twenty-three goldsmiths known to have been working in London in the 13th century, but the corresponding figure for the 14th century was fifty-seven.

These figures, though presumably not complete, argue a steady expansion of business, and the flourishing state of the silver trade evidently caused the authorities to realize that, whereas the ordinance of 1238 had stipulated a standard of quality, it had made no provision for ensuring that the standard was enforced.

An Act of Edward I in 1300 set out to make good this omission, and not only reiterated that silverware should be of the sterling standard, the same as the coinage, but also required that it should not leave the silversmiths' hands until it had been assayed by officials appointed by the fraternity of goldsmiths, and marked with a leopard's head as evidence that it was of the correct quality.

The year 1300 is therefore a milestone in the history of the craft, as it constituted the first step in the practice of hall-marking.

The Act was important for another reason, for whereas Henry II had imposed a fine on the goldsmiths for attempting to form an unlicensed guild, Edward I, by laying official duties upon them, tacitly acknowledged the existence of an organized association, and in these circumstances, it was clearly only a matter of time before this association would receive express legal recognition.

Accordingly, in 1327, Edward III granted the goldsmiths of London their first charter, thereby greatly enhancing their prestige and authority.

The wording of the grant places on record the requirement that goldsmiths were bound to carry on their business only in certain

[1] *English Goldsmiths and Their Marks*, 1921.

specific parts of the City of London, to facilitate the enforcement of the law, and alludes to the suspicion, amounting to a certainty, that some goldsmiths, who kept shops in obscure streets, bought vessels of gold and silver secretly without enquiring into the title of the vendor, and immediately melted them down.

These facts all bear witness to the increasing volume of trade in silverware, and suggest that secular patronage had become more important than ecclesiastical.

This seems to have prompted the government to take further steps to protect the public against actual or potential abuses, and in 1363, another statute of Edward III ordered that every master goldsmith should have a personal mark, which was to be struck on the piece after it had been assayed and stamped with the leopard's head—described in the Act as 'the King's Mark'. The object of this was presumably to enable any default to be brought home to the actual maker of a low-standard piece, which had managed to slip through the assay through the carelessness of the Warden.

STANDING CUPS

There is no doubt that for three hundred years from the beginning of the 14th century, the most important of all drinking vessels was the standing cup. Contemporary documents unfortunately give little assistance in ascertaining the precise nature of the silver vessels which are mentioned. What, for example, is one to make of the description 'chalispece' applied to a domestic silver vessel in a 14th-century will? It is evident from manuscripts, however, that for many years the most popular form of drinking cup was of the type represented by the Berwick St. James chalice of Plate 3a. Fig. 10, which is taken from the beautiful manuscript known as Queen Mary's Psalter, shows part of a festive scene in which precisely such a cup is being used by an enthusiastic toper, while Fig. 11 from the same source depicts the same sort of vessel employed in the celebration of the Mass.

One type of cup which received frequent mention in the Middle Ages was known as a Hanap. Various forms of the word

Fig. 10. 14th-century standing cup in use

Fig. 11. 14th-century chalice in use

were used among the French and Germanic peoples, and it occurred in Anglo-Saxon as *hnaepp*. The exact significance of the term cannot be determined beyond doubt, but it seems evident from the usual nature of the context that it was a large and important-looking standing cup with a cover. A number of silver drinking vessels presented to the Black Prince in 1371, for example, included 'one gilded hanap in the form of an acorn'.

Large covered cups in the 14th century seem to have been associated chiefly with important occasions or important people. Queen Mary's Psalter depicts a number of uncovered goblets in use at table, but one picture shows a king seated on a throne, while a kneeling servitor proffers a tall and imposing cup from which he has removed the cover, retaining it in his hand.

An example may be seen in Fig. 12, and it is probable that the term 'hanap' was applied to cups of this type. The stem was sometimes without a knop.

Some time in the course of the century under consideration another type of bowl was introduced for standing cups. This was taller and narrower than those discussed hitherto, and although it clearly derived its main inspiration from the beaker, something in its outline was strongly suggestive of a bell.

Bell-shaped bowls of modified shape were to be popular in the following century, but the only surviving 14th-century example is the tall ceremonial cup belonging to the Corporation of King's Lynn. The bowl and foot of this highly interesting vessel are decorated in enamel with figures in the costume of about 1350. Stripped of its ornament, the basic form of the bowl is as shown in Fig. 13.

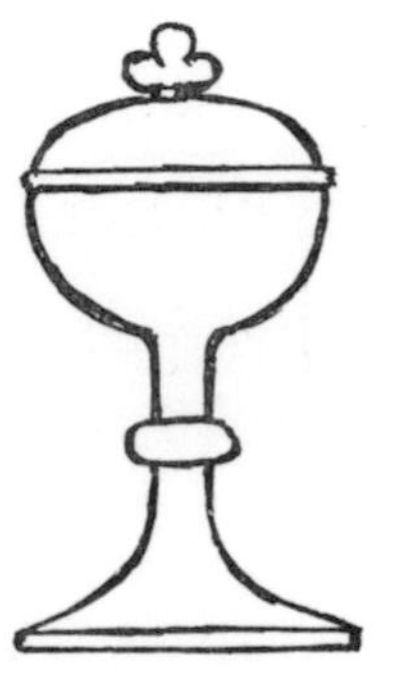

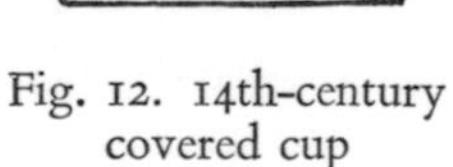

Fig. 12. 14th-century covered cup

Fig. 13. Bell-shaped bowl, 14th century

Fig. 14. 14th-century architectural stem

The shape of the straight, slender stem is noteworthy (Fig. 14), because whereas the stems of cups with the bird's-nest type of bowl merge into the spreading foot without interruption, the transition in the case of the King's Lynn cup is more sudden, and the two parts are shown as separate entities.

Many chalices of the period, and later, had round or polygonal stems of the same proportions, and being somewhat after the fashion of a slender column, may be regarded as an instance of the architectural feeling which affected many branches of applied art in the Middle Ages.

Many English chalices of the 14th and 15th centuries had feet which, instead of being circular, were cusped, or extended into a number of concave-sided points (Fig. 15), and although no English secular cups of the same design are known, it is probable that they existed at one time.

It has been suggested that this type of foot was introduced to prevent the chalice rolling about on the altar, when laid on its side on the conclusion of the Mass, but the formation in question often occurred in the details of woodwork, armour, and sculpture, and was simply an ingredient of the pervasive architectural feeling of the 14th and 15th centuries.

Fig. 15. Cusped foot of chalice

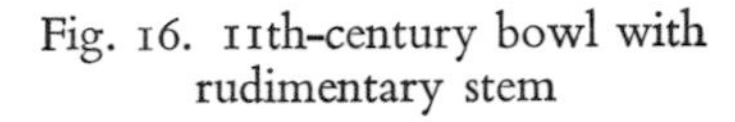

Fig. 16. 11th-century bowl with rudimentary stem

It would appear, therefore, that the fact that chalices with this sort of foot were unable to roll about was a convenience arising from the design, rather than its proximate cause. A picture from a French mediaeval manuscript, reproduced in volume 3 of *The Dictionary of English Furniture*,[1] shows a secular standing cup with a foot of precisely the same kind, and it is therefore more than likely that the same form occurred in England also.

DRINKING BOWLS

One of the figures in a banqueting scene in the Bayeux Tapestry is holding his drinking bowl in such a manner, that it seems evident that the vessel must have some kind of rudimentary stem (Fig. 16).

The Victoria and Albert Museum is fortunate in the possession of a later specimen in the same tradition, known as the Studley Bowl, from the circumstance that it belonged for a time to Studley Royal church in Yorkshire.

[1] Ralph Edwards, 1954.

This fine silver-gilt bowl may be seen in Plate 3b. Bowl and cover are engraved with foliage and the letters of an incomplete mediaeval alphabet, and this has led to the suggestion that it might have been made for a 14th-century child, the alphabet serving to teach him his letters while he ate his porridge. Apart from the obvious objection that an alphabet wanting several letters would give very imperfect instruction, it seems far more likely that the picturesque characters were used purely decoratively, as letters of the Arabic alphabet were sometimes used in Islamic countries, and furthermore, the weight of sheer mathematical probability is in favour of its having been intended as a drinking vessel.

The bowls of certain chalices of the period were of the same shape, and although it is likely that some secular cups were of the same type as these, none is known to have survived.

BEAKERS

It is evident from manuscript sources that beakers continued as popular as ever in the 14th century, some having either hemispherical or conical covers, but again, no existing specimens are known.

DRINKING HORNS

With drinking horns we are more fortunate, particularly as they were rather uncommon after the Norman Conquest.

Three 14th-century examples are known, and all of them show that silversmiths had solved the problem of instability by fitting two or more plain or fanciful legs to the horn, and to that extent, the vessel was far more convenient to use than it had ever been before. But it is evident from the comparative rarity with which drinking horns are mentioned in contemporary documents that they enjoyed no sort of popularity, and were probably used only on ceremonial occasions when it was desired to import a flavour of robust tradition. A 14th-century horn is shown in Fig. 17.

3a. 13th-century standing cup. *Height:* $5\frac{3}{4}''$
(*British Museum*)

3b. 14th-century drinking bowl. *Height:* $5\frac{1}{2}''$
(*Victoria and Albert Museum*)

4. 15th-century standing cup and cover. *Height:* $12\frac{3}{4}''$
(Christ's College Cambridge)

5a. 15th-century standing cup supported on talbots. *Height:* $5\frac{7}{8}''$
(by courtesy of the Historic Churches Preservation Trust)

5b. 15th-century standing cup on short stem. *Height:* $4\frac{1}{8}''$
(Victoria and Albert Museum)

6a. The Howard Grace Cup, mediaeval and Renaissance, 1525. *Height:* 12″
(*Victoria and Albert Museum*)

6b. Font-shaped cup, 1500. *Height:* $3\frac{3}{8}$″
(*Victoria and Albert Museum*)

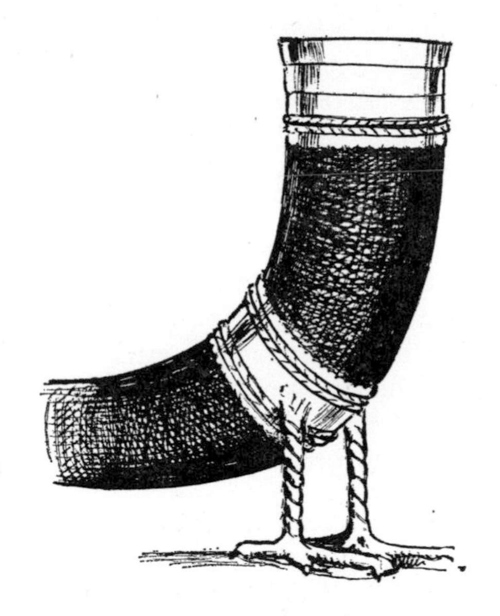

Fig. 17. 14th-century horn with feet

Fig. 18. 14th-century silver-mounted mazer

MAZERS

A mazer is a kind of drinking bowl of the familiar bird's-nest shape, fashioned out of wood. It seems clear from the derivation of the word that the originals of the species were made of burr-maple, but many of those still in existence show a very plain figure in the grain. No doubt the majority were quite unadorned, but the type concerns us here because a silver rim—

called a *cup-band*—and foot were often applied, and the centre of the internal base was frequently embellished with a circular silver boss, sometimes engraved, or decorated with enamel.

Mazers were mentioned as early as the 12th century, and almost certainly occurred very much earlier, but the oldest survivors, one of which is shown in Fig. 18, date from the 14th century.

The boss, or *print* as it is sometimes called, was decorated in various ways, which included formal floral motifs, heraldic devices, or something of a religious character, but it must not be assumed that the presence of the last-named always implies that the object bearing it came from a monastic refectory, because although mazers were undoubtedly popular in the abbeys, religious symbolism entered into the everyday lives of our mediaeval ancestors to a remarkable degree.

In spite of the statutes of 1300 and 1363, it is clear that in the last quarter of the 14th century the laws relating to assaying and marking were widely disregarded.

An Act of Richard II in 1378 attempted, though obviously with indifferent success, to ensure compliance with the law by providing that any offending silversmith should pay double the value of the vessel to an owner who complained to the authorities, and should be liable also to fine and imprisonment. However, in view of the fact that most surviving mediaeval plate is entirely unmarked, it seems likely that owners of unmarked pieces were often well content with their purchases, and so let the matter sleep.

THE 15TH CENTURY

STANDING CUPS

The type of drinking cup with wide, shallow bowl and spreading foot, already familiar from previous centuries, evidently continued into the 15th century with undiminished popularity in spite of the introduction of other designs. There were probably a good many made in the 14th century, and it is unreasonable to suppose that worthy vessels already in service would be abandoned or rewrought merely because new forms had been devised. Such destructive ideas were not to win favour for another hundred years.

Fig. 19. 15th-century shallow standing cups in use

Fig. 19 shows a convivial scene which is taken from the illuminated initial letter of a 15th-century drinking song, and two persons in it are shown with cups of 14th-century type.

One of those in the illustration has a knop in the stem, but some time in the first half of the century, cups began to appear with plain, trumpet-shaped stems and small feet, surmounted by receptacles which, while still owing some allegiance to the drinking bowl, were often deeper in relation to their width, and with a faint suggestion of angularity.

Probably the most distinguished example still in existence is the silver-gilt Foundress's Cup, of Christ's College, Cambridge, illustrated in Plate 4. Like most mediaeval plate it is unmarked, but certain heraldic charges inside the bowl fix its date, beyond doubt, as between 1435 and 1440.

Other cups of the period were naturally less elaborate, and some were of more squat appearance, but added height was sometimes given—as in the case of brass candlesticks of the same date—by supporting the foot of the cup on three or four small figures, such as lions or dogs.

An example of this may be seen in Plate 5a, which shows a cup of about 1450, with its foot resting on three talbots. It is still in use as a chalice, at Marston church, Oxford, but is known to have begun its existence as a secular drinking vessel in the possession of a wealthy Oxford bailiff.

Plate 5b shows another cup of the same basic type, but with an even shorter stem. As this vessel is almost identical with the lower part of the early 14th-century Ramsey Abbey censer in the Victoria and Albert Museum, it is possible that the type existed much earlier.

The trumpet-shaped stem seems to have remained the standard pattern until the beginning of the 16th century, and was not entirely superseded even then, but the bowls which it supported were of various types, one of the most important being in the form of a bell. A reference to this shape has been traced in the first quarter of the 15th century, and we have already considered a variant dating from the middle of the 14th century, but most known survivors appear to have been made after 1480.

A plain example of 1481 is among the plate of Pembroke College, Cambridge. It was at one time fitted with a cover, but this has been lost long since, as in the case of many other specimens of all periods. It is known as the 'Anathema' cup from a Latin inscription which it bears, calling down a curse on anyone who steals it. The type is shown in Fig. 20. A very beautiful example of the same species, decorated with a formalized plant motif, and displaying also the circuit of small silver balls at the junction of stem and bowl, is preserved in New College, Oxford.

In Fig. 21 is shown a modified form of the same general type as the foregoing, but the stem, though preserving more or less the trumpet outline, is embossed into bold lobes, and the bowl has taken on something of the semblance of a columbine flower. This cup, which has a somewhat German appearance, belongs to the last years of the 15th century.

Fig. 20. 15th-century cup with bell-shaped bowl

Fig. 21. Late 15th-century cup with embossed decoration

MAZERS

Silver-mounted mazers continued to be made in large numbers, many of them having bowls which were shallower than earlier ones, but with their capacity restored by deeper lip-bands. So great was the prestige of the standing cup, that some mazers were mounted on silver stems and feet of the prevailing design, as in Fig. 22, which also shows the deep silver band typical of the period.

BEAKERS

Only one English silver beaker of the 15th century still exists, and would seem to be of unusual pattern, as the lower part is surrounded with vertical ribs.[1] It may be assumed that many of

[1] See *English Domestic Silver*, C. Oman, 1947.

them were provided with covers, which in many cases probably had battlemented rims.

Fig. 22. 15th-century silver-mounted standing mazer

COCO-NUT CUPS

The trumpet stem, which was found so frequently on standing cups made entirely of silver, was also used for coco-nut cups, and several examples of these have survived from the 15th century. Though a coco-nut shell seems a rather obvious basis for a drinking vessel, it is difficult for us, in an age when international trade has made them commonplace, to understand the wonder and delight with which such exotics were regarded in the Middle Ages.

Fig. 23 illustrates a coco-nut cup of the 15th century. The decorated silver straps down the sides of the bowl were necessary to unite the rim with the top of the stem, and are very often found on vessels made of brittle non-metallic substances mounted in silver.

Fig. 23. 15th-century silver-mounted coco-nut cup

An Act of Edward IV in 1477 referred to the leopard's head as being 'crowned', and it may be presumed that this addition to the mark was introduced in the year of the statute. The same Act made the entire body of London goldsmiths responsible for any dereliction of duty on the part of the Warden, whose task it was to strike the mark on plate. It appears thereupon, that the goldsmiths, by a private regulation of their own not imposed by law, decided to introduce another mark to enable them to obtain indemnity from the man actually responsible.

This took the form of a letter of the alphabet, to be changed annually, the first being the Lombardic letter A for 1478.

As they knew the identity of the Warden for any particular year, it may be presumed that the introduction of the date-letter achieved its purpose, but its chief importance for us lies in the fact that it enables us to determine, within a little, the date of manufacture of any piece of fully-marked plate submitted for assay since the late 15th century.

CHAPTER TWO

THE TUDOR PERIOD

1500–1600

After 1500, the mediaeval style continued for a time with silverware no less than with architecture and furniture, and probably did not die out entirely until about the middle of the 16th century.

It is clear, however, that a new spirit was abroad much earlier than this, though it cannot be said with certainty when it first made its influence felt, particularly as the wholesale melting of plate which took place during the Civil War may well have involved the destruction of some early 16th-century vessels designed or decorated in the Renaissance manner.

The Renaissance style, which began to reach England between 1500 and 1525, was derived, not directly from classical originals, but at second-hand from Italian traditions which were introduced chiefly *via* Germany and the Netherlands. While it was more classical in its details than in its general feeling, it was nevertheless totally different from the Gothic style, which owed its distinctive character to the incidentals of mediaeval architecture.

It is sometimes assumed that the new style was brought into England by Hans Holbein the younger, who, in addition to his other artistic activities, was a distinguished designer of silver drinking vessels. But Holbein did not reach England until 1526, and although there can be little doubt that he helped to popularize the German version of the Renaissance manner, it was undoubtedly already in the country before he arrived.

It seems probable that it was the introduction of the new

fashions which was responsible, more than anything else, for the disappearance of much of the mediaeval domestic silver which had survived the 15th century.

The tendency to form large accumulations of plate became more widespread than ever in the 16th century, and penetrated into sections of society which it had previously left unaffected, but the collections owned by certain prelates and nobles must have been immense, often involving a corresponding destruction of old plate to provide the raw material for the new.

In his account of the life of Cardinal Wolsey, George Cavendish, the cardinal's gentleman-usher, gives the impression that he considered the modernity of some of his master's plate as a recommendation. He refers, for example, to a 'cupbord . . . full of gilt plate, very sumptious, and of the newest facions.'

The following passage from the same work gives a remarkable picture of the quantity of objects in precious metal surrendered by Wolsey to the King, after his fall from office in 1529.

'Than had he in ii Chambers adioynyng to the Gallery, the one called the gylt Chamber, and thother called most Commenly the Councell Chamber, wherin ware sett in eche, ii brode & long tables vppon trestelles, where vppon was sett suche a nomber of plate of all sortes as ware all most Incredyble. In the gylt Chamber was sett owt vppon the tables nothyng but all gylt plate. And vppon a Cupbord standyng vnder a wyndowe was garnysshed all holy wt plate of cleane gold, whereof Somme was sett wt peerle & riche stones. And in the Councell chamber was sett all wyght plate & parcell gylt. And vnder the tables in bothe the Chambers ware sett baskettes wt old plate w^che^ was not estemed but for broken plate & old, not worthy to be occupied.'

Apart from their antiquarian interest, the despised contents of those baskets would now be worth a king's ransom, but it is clear that Wolsey was yielding up, not so much his household utensils, as his investments.

The greater part of the plate alluded to by Cavendish probably consisted of drinking vessels and vessels designed for the service of wine and beer, and his reference to plate which was set with pearls and rich stones brings us to a consideration of an interesting standing cup in the Victoria and Albert Museum, known as the Howard Grace Cup.

STANDING CUPS

This example, which is shown in Plate 6a, is made of ivory, with jewelled silver-gilt mounts bearing the date-letter for 1525. It forms a battleground between the Renaissance and Gothic styles, with the latter fighting a rearguard action.

The bands of ornament round the foot, the rim of the cover, and the base of the finial, may be clearly identified as being in the Renaissance style, while on the other hand, the figure of St. George which surmounts the cover is wearing armour of the late 15th century, and the pierced gallery a short distance below the bowl is entirely mediaeval in character.

Though of great stylistic interest, it is a somewhat graceless vessel in spite of its name, but the proportions were no doubt conditioned partly by the shape of the piece of ivory which forms the receptacle.

A new type of drinking vessel which had no apparent connection with the Renaissance, and yet was probably unknown in the 15th century, was the font-shaped cup.

An example of the year 1500 is shown in Plate 6b, and although a number are still in existence, this is the earliest one known. There is obviously a basic connection between cups of this sort and other stemmed drinking bowls such as the 15th-century example in Plate 5b, the short, trumpet-shaped stem being common to both, but font-shaped cups may be readily identified by the wide, straight-sided bowls, which had never occurred before.

Seven vessels of this kind are known to have survived, some of them being equipped with covers. The Worshipful Company of Goldsmiths own a magnificent, but almost entirely plain example of 1503; it is complete with its original cover, which greatly alters the total aspect of the piece and gives it an added importance (Fig. 24). They were not always plain, and a specimen which bears the date-letter for 1515, in the possession of one of the Oxford colleges, is decorated with a pineapple design.

Font-shaped cups were made for three-quarters of a century, and although the comparatively small number of survivors makes it impossible to draw any exact deductions as to the period of their greatest incidence, it seems likely, in view of the archaic character of the design and the competition offered by other types, that they were most popular in the first half of the 16th century.

Fig. 24. Early 16th-century font-shaped cup with cover

A related type existed at the same time, though it probably first appeared slightly later. This is generally called simply a Flat Cup. The bowl was similar to the font shape, but with an everted rim, and the stem, though broad and stout, was very considerably higher. An excellent example of 1551 is preserved in Deane church, Hampshire, and another, made a few years later, is among the large collection of English plate in the Kremlin.

Mazers began to decline in popularity as the century advanced, probably because improved economic conditions resulted in a wider distribution of wealth, which enabled silver-mounted vessels of humble wood to be eschewed in favour of cups made wholly of silver. Sometimes, the non-metallic body of a vessel would be replaced by a silver one of the same size and shape, and it must not be assumed that this was invariably due to the fact that the original had become damaged or broken.

As mentioned in the previous chapter, standing mazers, with mounts and stems of silver, probably began to appear in the second half of the 15th century. The Barber-Surgeons' Company were presented with a particularly fine example by Henry VIII, and although it is perhaps unlikely that barbers are often made fellows of the Royal College of Surgeons nowadays, the King's gift was made in celebration of the union of the two bodies in 1540.

The hall-marks show that this vessel was made in 1523, but the replacement of the wooden receptacle by a silver one is believed to have been carried out by the King's goldsmith just before it was presented to the Company.

This interesting standing cup, which is illustrated in Plate 7a, was seen by Samuel Pepys at Surgeons' Hall in 1663. He records that everyone who drank from it had to shake it to make the bells ring: a piece of puerility in keeping with the appearance of the bells, which greatly detract from an otherwise dignified and well-proportioned vessel.

It is a somewhat unusual cup, as might be expected of a royal gift, but certain identification factors may be noted nevertheless. The original lip-band of the bowl, with its invected border, is late Gothic in style, but the overall foliate decoration, the circuit of short gadroons at the base of the stem, and the scroll brackets below the bowl, are all of a typically Renaissance character. The last should be especially noted, as they were to persist, in varying degrees of sophistication, well into the 17th century. They most probably derived from the pinched serpentine brackets on the stems of many Venetian glasses, which were beginning to enjoy an increasing prestige in England in the first half of the 16th century.

In addition to the influence exerted by Holbein, and certain Italians and other foreigners who were busy about the King's palaces, another very important source of Renaissance decoration was the engraved sheets of ornament, issuing from various

German centres, based on designs by Virgil Solis, Hans Brosamer, and other artists.

In general, these designs were freely adapted by English silversmiths, whose consequent work still preserved a thoroughly native character, but occasionally a drinking vessel was found approximating very closely to one of the German designs.

An example is furnished by the silver-gilt Boleyn Cup, in Plate 7b, which belongs to Cirencester church. Apart from the cover, it has a strong similarity to a cup designed by Hans Brosamer.

The chief features to note, apart from the shape, which appears to be based on that of certain contemporary Venetian wine glasses, are the heavy gadroons on the stem and the lower part of the straight-funnel bowl, and the acanthus leaves above and below the knop and round the rim of the foot. The cover is surmounted by the personal badge of Anne Boleyn as Queen, and there is a convincing tradition that the cup, which is over twelve inches high, was once her property.

A drinking vessel which was very popular in Germany in the 16th and early 17th centuries was the standing beaker. It had the usual flaring cylindrical body with an almost flat base, mounted on a stem and foot. A few exist in England, though there is usually some doubt about their national origin, and the type seems, strangely enough, to have failed to impress the English to any extent, but the undoubtedly English cup shown in Fig. 25 represents an approach to the beaker-form.

It will be seen that the tall bowl is in the shape of an elongated bell, and not at all like that of a normal beaker which stands on its own base. It can be said, however, that it has some claim to be considered as a standing beaker on account of the height of the bowl in relation to its width.

The reader will recognize the Renaissance character of the decoration, but it is unusual for a large, separate calix of acanthus leaves to be used to support the receptacle in such a very functional manner. This is virtually an early instance of the so-called cut-card work, which will be considered in Chapter 4. The cup bears the hall-mark for 1545.

A 4th-century gold cup of similar proportions forms part of the Osztropataka hoard preserved in the Kunsthistorisches Museum in Vienna, and although it often happened that European forms eventually became naturalized in England, the type in question seems to have been an exception. Apart from the shape, however, the decorative treatment of the cup in Fig. 25 is typically English of the 16th century.

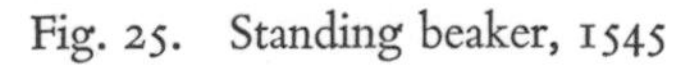

Fig. 25. Standing beaker, 1545

Fig. 26. Standing cup with beaker-type bowl

Fig. 26 illustrates a standing cup made about five years earlier than the one just discussed. The round-funnel bowl is also manifestly based on the beaker-form, but is less dominant than in the previous example. The foot is embossed with widely-spaced gadroons, and these are answered on the base of the bowl, not with gadroons, but with a calix of solid, vertical ribs in which the bowl rests. This was an unusual feature in English silver, though it was often found on Spanish vessels in the following century, but attention has been drawn to it here because we shall be meeting it again very much later.

The term 'sterling silver' implies the presence of no less than 92·5 per cent pure silver, and no more than 7·5 per cent. alloy. When Henry VIII debased the coinage in 1544, it consisted of only half silver and half alloy, and the following year became even worse.

This seems to have prompted the goldsmiths to seek some means of reassuring the buying public as to the standard of wrought plate, which remained of the original quality. They no doubt considered that as the King's Mark had been compromised by the King himself in corrupting his own coinage, it would be advisable to introduce another mark which would remove any suspicion that the metal used by the silversmiths had been treated in the same way.

The device selected was apparently taken from the royal arms of England, and consisted of a crowned lion passant guardant. The crown was used only from 1544 to 1549, but although the coinage was restored to the sterling standard by Queen Elizabeth in 1560, the lion passant continued to be used to denote sterling silver. As the leopard's head (or lion's face) had had its original function usurped by the lion passant, it eventually came to be recognized as the mark of the London Assay Office.

There seems little doubt that the debasement of the currency served as a powerful stimulant to the production of all kinds of silver vessels, as it was obviously better that investments should be in the form of handsome objects of reliable quality, rather than bags of coins which were little more than tokens.

Before the end of Henry VIII's reign, covered standing cups of imposing and monumental appearance began to be made in comparatively large numbers.

The usual type of bowl was somewhat like a thistle, the upper part being in the form of a beaker, but with a swelling protuberance at its base. The form was of late classical origin, and we shall be meeting it again in the early 19th century.

In general, the stem consisted substantially of a miniature pot or vase of silver, apparently known at the time as the 'potkin'. This was most commonly decorated with scroll brackets such as those which we have already seen on the standing mazer of the Barber-Surgeons.

Fig. 27. Standing cup with thistle-shaped bowl, pre-1550

An example of the 1540s is illustrated in Fig. 27. Apart from other kinds of typical Renaissance ornament which it bears, the swelling at the base of the bowl is chased with a form of decoration frequently found on furniture of the period, and consisting of the small medallion portraits often known as 'Romayne Heads'.

Cups with the thistle type of bowl persisted with a less concave profile until the early part of the 17th century, some of the later

7a. Standing mazer with silver bowl, 1523. *Height:* $10\frac{1}{2}''$
(by courtesy of the Barber-Surgeons' Company and Goldsmiths' Company)

7b. The Boleyn Cup, 1535. *Height:* $12\frac{1}{2}''$
(by courtesy of the Historic Churches Preservation Trust)

8a. Elizabethan ostrich-egg cup. *Height:* $8\frac{1}{2}''$
(*Mr. J. F. Hayward*)

8b. Elizabethan cup of agate. *Height:* $7\frac{7}{8}''$
(*Victoria and Albert Museum*)

ceremonial ones being profusely decorated, but they were not always entirely of silver.

The Worshipful Company of Goldsmiths possess a gilt example of 1545, the tall, polygonal bowl being carved out of rock crystal, and resting in a projecting gadrooned cup, which is united to the wide silver rim of the vessel by three vertical straps of the same metal. The base of the potkin stands on the top of another piece of carved crystal in the form of a hat, and is joined to the foot by three decorated scroll brackets which arch over the crystal. The cup almost certainly had a cover at one time, but this has now disappeared, as is often the case. For a long time, it was supposed that crystal had the power of detecting poison.

Coco-nut cups continued to be fashionable until the middle of the 17th century. The silver mounts were of the same character as those on other contemporary cups, but specimens are sometimes found with the nut elaborately carved in harmony with the decoration of the silver.

They must have been cheaper than their counterparts in precious metal, but the dramatic tonal contrast between the dark, polished shell, and the beautifully wrought silver-gilt mounts, often gives an effect of great richness.

When the fortunes of the owner of a coco-nut cup improved, or if the nut suffered some injury, it would sometimes be replaced by a silver receptacle of the same kind. An example of this is furnished by the celebrated Goodricke Cup in the British Museum. Its silver-gilt mounts bear the hall-mark for 1563, but the body of the piece is in white silver, engraved in a manner typical of the first quarter of the 17th century.

Though their graceful, voluted shape must have made them somewhat inconvenient for use as drinking vessels, silver-mounted standing cups were also made of nautilus shells (Fig. 28). The effect is one of ethereal, pearly daintiness, but survivors are exceedingly rare owing to the fragility of the material. Most specimens encountered are likely to have originated in either of the great German metal-working centres of Augsburg or Nürnberg rather than in England.

Cups made from large, silver-mounted eggshells receive

mention in mediaeval documents, but the earliest ostrich-egg cups still in existence date from the 16th century. Plate 8a illustrates a finely decorated silver-gilt specimen in the collection of Mr. J. F. Hayward; it is unmarked, but was made in about 1560.

Apart from the difference in colour, all such cups have much the same appearance as those made from coco-nut shells, but the

Fig. 28. 16th-century nautilus-shell cup; detail

slightly pockmarked texture of the eggshell makes it seem almost like a ceramic substance.

It is recorded that in 1573 the Archbishop of Canterbury presented Queen Elizabeth with 'oone sault of agth garnished with golde'.

Salts, or salt-cellars, were not the only objects made of agate in the 16th century, and Plate 8b shows a wine cup, mounted in silver-gilt, with a bowl carved out of a solid piece of oriental agate.

The shape is strangely suggestive of that of a wine glass of the mid-19th century, but although the polished, translucent hard-stone had great beauty of its own the vessel is of interest chiefly because of the mounts, which bear marks showing that the silver was assayed in 1567.

Several Renaissance elements are discernible: lions' masks, dolphins, and short radial gadroons. The foot is surmounted by a very Germanic form of embellishment in the shape of carefully modelled, naturalistic snails.

The metalwork as a whole is typical of the worst and best aspects of contemporary German design. In general, Teutonic designers seem to have been more concerned with ornament than with shape, and the cluttered appearance of the stem and foot of this cup almost succeeds in vitiating the graceful basic form altogether. But of the superb quality of the craftsmanship displayed in all the details, there can be no doubt whatever.

In various antiquarian fields, collectors and dealers often make use of a jargon of their own which is sometimes inaccurate and misleading.

An example of this is the word *tazza*, which is simply the Italian for 'cup', but it is frequently applied, quite inappropriately, to flat dishes, and salvers supported on central stems.

There is, however, one type of silver vessel for which its use is perfectly legitimate, and as the term serves to distinguish the cup in question from other kinds, there is no reason why it should not be retained.

A tazza of 1564 is illustrated in Plate 9a. A feature that is common to all members of the species is the wide, shallow bowl with low, curving sides, which is quite different in section from that of the more angular font-shaped cup, but there is some variation in the form of the stems.

The cylindrical type, with central annular knop like the one illustrated, seems to have been the most popular in England, but others had stems consisting chiefly of potkins, treated as a rule rather simply, while a well-known example of 1532, sold at Sotheby's in 1957, had a short, wide stem of modified trumpet shape, with a small amount of Renaissance decoration. Late in the century, the stem might consist of a simple inverted baluster, lightly engraved.

The treatment of the foot of the specimen illustrated in Plate 9a would enable us to assign the cup to the Elizabethan period apart from other identification factors. The ornament, which is entirely Germanic in character, consists of masks and lumpy fruits in fairly high relief, the second in particular being very common until after 1600; we shall be meeting it again on another kind of drinking vessel.

Some tazzas were inordinately wide and shallow, and it seems evident that these should be regarded, not as standing cups to contain wine, but rather as standing dishes to contain fruit; they are often shown performing this function in contemporary and later pictures.

Those of more reasonable size were probably used for either purpose, according to the caprice of the owner. Although they must have been somewhat inconvenient as containers for liquor, in that the slightest awkward movement would cause the wine to slop over the edge of the bowl, it is evident from classical mural decorations and Dutch paintings that their classification as drinking vessels is correct.

In the second half of the 16th century, there were signs that the highly-ornamented German style was beginning to wane in popularity in favour of one which was more truly English in feeling—a style, in fact, which relied for its effect more on form than surface decoration.

This represented the inception of a tendency which was to persist through the first half of the 17th century up to the Restoration, and for this reason, is often considered to owe its existence to the spread of puritanism. Although, however, this may have been a contributory factor, it seems more likely that it was due rather to a reaction in public taste, which while it may well have been increasingly strengthened and sustained by the Puritans' dislike for any form of ostentation in art, had its origin in aesthetic, rather than religious considerations.

Plate 9b illustrates a celebrated silver-gilt standing cup in the new, simple style, preserved in the British Museum. It was made in 1573 for Sir Nicholas Bacon, who was appointed Lord Keeper of the Great Seal in 1558 on the accession of Queen Elizabeth. The source of the metal was the obsolete Great Seal of Mary Tudor and Philip of Spain.

Many cups of the same kind were made at the same period, nearly all of them having stems of similar form, with an inverted baluster as the main feature. The bowls varied to some extent, both in height and width, one kind being shaped like the more pointed half of an egg, but whatever the relationship between the two dimensions, the outline always had the same subtle curvature.

Fig. 29. Late 16th-century wine cup

Very little decoration was used, and sometimes none at all. It consisted, for the most part, of simple engraving or flat chasing either in the form of widely-spaced floral and foliate scrolls, or thin parallel lines placed closely enough together to give parts of the cup a matt appearance.

Some were without covers, but all of them, covered or uncovered, give the impression that they were individual wine cups intended for use rather than for display.

The same could be said, with complete certainty, of an even simpler form of cup introduced in the last years of the century. The bowls were generally of round-funnel shape, and the stems consisted primarily of inverted balusters of very slim build.

An example is shown in Fig. 29. These cups remained popular well into the 17th century, and the various changes which took place in their appearance will be considered later.

We have now discussed all the more important types of standing cup current in the 16th century, but there were several others, of varying degrees of rarity, which may be briefly mentioned.

We have already alluded, in the previous chapter, to a 14th-century reference to a gilded hanap 'in the form of an acorn', but the earliest surviving examples date from the 16th century, and even these are extremely rare.

The stem sometimes took the form of the trunk of an oak tree with one or more short, severed branches, while the bulging lower part of the bowl was embossed to represent the projections on an acorn-cup, and the upper part, completed with a dome-shaped cover with button finial, formed the acorn itself. There is an example of 1585 in the Museum of Fine Arts in Boston, Massachusetts, and a fine specimen in solid gold, with a foot typical of the early 17th century, was formerly in the possession of Stapleford church, Leicestershire.

Apart from the thistle-shaped cup, which achieved a great deal of popularity in England, other designs introduced from Germany were less successful. Among these were drinking vessels in the form of gourds, melons, and birds.

The bowl of a gourd-shaped cup is shown in Fig. 30. In all probability most of them were originally equipped with covers, and although they are handsome enough, one can never be quite certain whether they are English or German, even though they may bear full sets of English hall-marks.

It has been established that numbers of German cups were

imported unmarked, and subsequently assayed and stamped at Goldsmiths' Hall. They were also struck with the mark of the silversmith who submitted them for assay, so that in the absence of collateral evidence, their nationality must always be a matter of doubt. A good specimen bearing the English hall-marks for 1585 is in the possession of the Armourers' and Brasiers' Company of London.

Fig. 30. Bowl of gourd-shaped cup, late 16th century

Fig. 31. Bowl of melon-shaped cup, late 16th century

Cups in the form of melons probably satisfied the German fondness for gadrooning. The natural convexities and concavities in the body of a melon were, in the silver version, increased in number, making a series of vertical gadroons which rose up the sides of the globular vessel, and met at the finial-crowned apex of the domed cover which completed the sphere (Fig. 31).

An example of 1563, among the collection of plate belonging to the Inner Temple, has a coiled foot and stem representing the stalk of the melon, rising up to the base of the bowl, somewhat after the fashion of a rearing serpent. The spaces between the coils are spanned, here and there, by spiral tendrils. The cup as a whole gives the impression that the designer was unable to make up his mind whether to make a good standing cup or a good model of a melon.

The same considerations may be said to apply to cups in the form of falcons, or other birds. The creature was usually represented standing on an oblong plinth with wings folded. The head of the bird formed the cover, which was detachable at the neck, and although the craftsman often went to a great deal of trouble, talons, feathers, and other detail being rendered with the utmost fidelity, the result was generally neither a convenient drinking vessel nor a satisfying piece of sculpture.

One of the Livery Companies of the City of London possesses no less than five of these cups, but they were always made to special order, and are understandably rare.

DRINKING BOWLS

It is not easy to determine to what extent silver drinking bowls were used in the 16th century, as although their existence is attested by contemporary documents, in which they are sometimes referred to as being in 'nests', it is possible that the term 'bowl' may often mean nothing more than a mazer, or sometimes a standing cup with a bowl-shaped receptacle. At all events, surviving specimens are exceedingly rare.

Various kinds of silver-mounted bowls, such as wooden mazers, and others made of marble or alabaster, were deeper than earlier examples, and usually had the silver rim and foot united by vertical straps like those on coco-nut or ostrich-egg cups of the same period. They may all be identified as belonging to the 16th century by the style of the mounts.

BEAKERS

Beakers undoubtedly continued to be popular in the 16th century throughout the post-Gothic period, but although no early Elizabethan examples appear to exist, it is known that they were in precisely the same style as later ones, including those made in the early 17th century.

They were six or seven inches high, the cylindrical bodies curving outwards near the top, and generally with a spreading foot-ring soldered to the base. The foot-ring was almost invariably decorated with small-scale Renaissance ornament, such as short gadroons, egg-and-dart, or leafage, applied by means of repeating dies.

The decoration on the bodies consisted mostly of engraved floral scrolls, often enclosed between strapwork bands below the rim, coats of arms, and formalized vases of flowers all confined to the upper half of the beaker. While it cannot be pretended that the engraving was of a very distinguished character, at least it had the merit of relieving the plainness of the surface without in any way impairing the form of the vessel. An example is shown in Fig. 32.

Fig. 32. Elizabethan beaker

A very rare type, known as a Magdalen cup, had a strongly German appearance. It differed from ordinary beakers in that the base of the body was slightly recessed, then swelled out again to form a foot. One of these cups is in the possession of Honington church, Lincolnshire.

In addition to individual beakers, others were made in nests of as many as ten. Each vessel had an applied horizontal moulding encircling the body near the top, and this rested upon the rim of the one below. The topmost beaker usually had a domed cover.

The Germans were very attached to various kinds of double cups, in which one was inverted over another, identical except at the rim. The upper of the two thus formed a cover, which kept out the dust when they were not in use.

An ostensibly English example, bearing the London hall-marks for 1572, is in the Hermitage Museum, Leningrad. It consists of two beakers, each embellished with applied hoops and engraved staves, so that when placed together they form a long wine-barrel in miniature. This double beaker has a certain amount of typically English engraving, but a very similar specimen in the Victoria and Albert Museum bears German hall-marks, and engraving may be applied at any time after a vessel is finished.

POTS

In the will of Sir John Montacute, dated 1388, the following bequests occur: 'to my sons John and Thomas two gilt pots . . . to my daughter Alianore a gilt cup.'

It is evident from this that a pot was something different from a cup, though it gives no clue as to its precise nature.

A clearer picture begins to emerge from a passage in Cavendish's *Life of Cardinal Wolsey*: 'Every chamber had a bason & an yewer of silver, & some cleare gylt & some parcell gylt, & some ii great potts of silver in lyke manere, and oon pott at the least with wyne and beare, a boll or coblett, and a silver pott to drynk bere.'

Here we have a reference to two sorts of silver pots: one sort to contain wine or beer, and another from which the beer was drunk.

It is obvious that the pots containing the bulk supply were serving-vessels, in other words, what were known in the 16th century as 'livery pots' (French *livrer*—to deliver). These were provided with handles and covers, as they had been since early mediaeval times. We may probably assume then, that the pot for drinking beer was a smaller individual vessel of the same kind.

For a long time, there appears to have been no sort of convention ruling the use of various kinds of pots, the choice being at the discretion of the drinker, so that a smaller vessel convenient for serving wine might be used for drinking beer and *vice versa*, and even a very large pot might sometimes be employed for drinking.

Habits in these matters were no doubt international, and an early 16th-century woodcut by Albrecht Dürer depicts a woman in the act of taking a hearty swig from a pot holding about three-quarters of a gallon, while another shows a smaller pot of the usual tankard variety being used for pouring liquor into a beaker.

It is clear from these facts that the popular division of handled pots of reasonable size into jugs and tankards is not only arbitrary, but misleading, in view of the general modern significance of the word 'jug', and as we are concerned here with drinking vessels, the author proposes to describe as 'tankards' all such vessels dating from and after the middle years of the 16th century, whether they served two purposes or one only. As none has survived from the early part of the century, we shall have no occasion to meddle with them.

TANKARDS

In the Middle Ages, the word 'tankard' was applied to a large wooden pot for carrying water, equipped with a cover and handle, and 'tanggard pots' of pewter were mentioned in 1482,[1] but the term does not appear to have been used in relation to a silver drinking vessel until the mid-16th century, although, as already indicated, such vessels undoubtedly existed before.

The earliest type of silver tankard still in existence had a body which was globular in the lower part, narrowing into a wide,

[1] *Antique Pewter of the British Isles*, Ronald F. Michaelis, 1955.

tapering cylinder which flared out at the rim. An expansive foot-ring was soldered to the base.

The hollow handle was of D-section with the flat side outward, wrought out of sheet silver; it was soldered to the top of the vessel near the rim, and again to the most protuberant part, thereafter curving away from the body so that its shape was that of a modified letter S. With slight variation, this remained the standard type of handle for tankards throughout their long history.

Fig. 33. Tankard, mid-16th century; the earliest type

The cover, or lid, was in the form of a low, flattened dome, with a horizontally-flanged edge extending back to the top of the handle to which it was hinged. A cast, vertical thumb-piece enabled the lid to be swung backward for filling or drinking. Most were quite plain, apart from slight engraving.

An example of the period is illustrated in Fig. 33. It will be seen that it is based on a very ancient form of pottery vessel, only instead of being moulded, or thrown on a wheel, the body was raised by hammering, in spite of its complicated shape, from a flat disc of sheet silver.

Other silver tankards of the second half of the 16th century were of two main kinds. One had a body consisting of an almost true cylinder, narrow in relation to its height, and the other was rather shorter and wider, but tapered from base to rim. In the following century, larger varieties of the first began to be called flagons.

Fig. 34. Tall cylindrical tankard, Elizabethan

These straight-sided tankards were very often decorated in a manner typical of the period, and the flagon type sometimes had a more ornate kind of handle as in Fig. 34. Large numbers of these tankards were made in Germany at the same time.

In Plate 10a is shown an example of the other sort of tankard, which was probably more popular owing to its more convenient height, its greater stability, and its more English appearance. The reader will have no difficulty in identifying the high relief, embossed ornament as Elizabethan.

The two projecting horizontal mouldings encircling the body should be noted, because they were highly typical of the period. Sometimes, the upper of the two might be omitted, and the lower one replaced by a much finer cabled wire soldered to the body, and embellished with minute, widely-spaced winged heads or masks at regular intervals.

The lid was invariably in the form of a high dome, surmounted by a finial, and the presence of the thumb-piece indicates that the finial was not essential for raising the lid, but owed its presence to the example furnished by covered standing cups.

As might be expected from our experience of standing cups, tankards were also frequently made of substances other than precious metal, mounted in silver or silver-gilt.

It is recorded that on one of Queen Elizabeth's periodic progresses through the country, from which she seldom returned worse off than when she started, Lady Cobham presented her with 'oone tankerde of allablaster garnished with silver and guilt'. Various kinds of marble tankards were made up to the early 17th century, though they were probably never very popular owing to their great weight, particularly when filled with beer.

Glass was also used, and Plate 10b illustrates an example in the British Museum made of Venetian enamel-glass. It will be observed that it is similar in shape to the bulbous silver tankard in Fig. 33. The silver-gilt mounts bear the hall-marks for 1548.

Chinese porcelain vases of convenient size were occasionally converted into tankards by the addition of silver foot-rings, neck-bands, handles, and lids, and an example illustrated in Fig. 35 shows that the transformation has been unable to disguise the Oriental shape of the vessel. A vogue existed at the same time for silver-mounted porcelain wine jugs.

Marble, Venetian glass, and porcelain were all materials enjoying a high degree of esteem, but not everyone could afford them. There is no doubt that the most popular of all non-metallic tankards with silver mounts were made of pottery, either native or German, the vast majority consisting of the mottled brown stoneware from the Rhineland, now known, rather unaccountably, as 'tigerware', though the markings are far more suggestive of the skin of a leopard.

These pots are usually described as jugs, but as they were undoubtedly drinking vessels rather than serving vessels, it is more reasonable to call them tankards.

Fig. 35. Elizabethan silver-mounted porcelain tankard

In 1558, a French priest named Etienne Perlin visited England, and left an interesting, though somewhat anti-English account of his experiences. Since he records, however, that he was often addressed as 'France dogue,'' and 'or son', we should perhaps rather commend his restraint than rail at his censures.

He had the following comments to make: 'As to the way of life of the English, they are somewhat impolite, for they belch at the table without reserve or shame, even before persons of the greatest dignity. They consume great quantities of beer, double and single, and drink it, not out of glasses, but from earthen pots with handles and covers of silver, even in the houses of persons of medium wealth, and as for the poor, the covers of their pots are only of pewter, and in some villages their beer pots are made of wood.'

Perlin's account provides striking evidence of the vast numbers of silver-mounted stoneware tankards used in the 16th century, though he was not quite correct in saying that the handles were made of silver. They were made of pottery, but were often overlaid with silver. A richly-ornamented specimen of this kind, dating from about 1560, is shown in Plate 11a.

An interesting example, preserved at Sudeley Castle, Gloucestershire, has a body consisting of a small, wide-mouthed stoneware pot, bearing the sort of crude, bearded face popularly supposed to be a likeness of the learned Jesuit, Cardinal Bellarmino.

TWO-HANDLED CUPS

In the early days of the Church in England, when the sacrament was still administered to the laity in both kinds, it was sometimes found convenient to use chalices of large size, and these were often provided with two handles, one opposite the other.

Mediaeval livery pots sometimes displayed the same feature, but little is known of secular drinking vessels, similarly equipped, until the 17th century when they became very numerous.

Fig. 36. Two-handled cup, early 16th century

9a. Tazza, 1564. *Height:* $5\frac{7}{8}''$

(*Victoria and Albert Museum*)

9b. Wine cup and cover, 1573. *Height:* $11\frac{2}{5}''$

(*British Museum*)

10a. Elizabethan cylindrical tankard. *Height:* $7\frac{1}{4}''$
(by courtesy of the Goldsmiths' Company)

10b. Silver-mounted glass tankard, 1548. *Height:* $5\frac{4}{5}''$
(British Museum)

Fig. 36 shows a type of two-handled cup or pot which existed in the second quarter of the 16th century, and an inventory dating from 1595 refers to 'silver potts w[t] eares', which were probably of similar design. Others, existing at the same time, were taller in the neck, and with less protuberant lower parts.

A contemporary expression for setting the arms akimbo was 'to make the pot with the two ears', clearly based on a fancied resemblance between human arms and the handles of the pot, and as the swelling form of these vessels was somewhat suggestive of the human pelvic region, we may probably assume that they were also the type sometimes described at the time as 'haunch pots'. When the latter are mentioned in contemporary documents, their weights are often given, and it is evident from these that some of them were of a size appropriate to an individual drinking vessel.

The Renaissance character of the cup shown in Fig. 36 is very apparent, and as its inspiration must have come originally from Italy, it seems almost incredible that another Italian or Byzantine type should not have been known in England at the same time.

The latter is represented by the silver-mounted crystal cup illustrated in Fig. 37. This is said to be of 12th-century date,

Fig. 37. Silver-mounted crystal two-handled cup, 12th century

and is preserved in the Treasury of St. Mark's, Venice. It was a shape that was destined to be highly favoured in the 17th century, but unfortunately, no 16th-century examples are known.

It is difficult to arrive at a just estimate of the extent to which silver drinking vessels were used for their ostensible purpose in the

16th century, or the extent to which they were treated primarily as investments, satisfying, at the same time, a taste for lavish display.

The evidence sometimes appears contradictory. Etienne Perlin, who, as mentioned previously, visited England in 1558, wrote: 'Please to remember that in this country they commonly use silver vessels when they drink wine'.

On the other hand, William Harrison, writing in 1587, said: 'It is a world to see in these our days, wherein gold and silver most aboundeth, how that our gentility, as loathing those metals (because of the plenty) do now generally choose rather the Venice glasses, both for our wine and beer, than any of those metals or stone wherein before time we have been accustomed to drink.'

The same writer makes it clear, however, that his statement is not to be taken as universally true even in regard to the 'gentility', for he says in another place: 'As for drink it is usually filled in pots, goblets, jugs, bowls of silver, in noblemen's houses'.

The truth probably lay, as usual, somewhere between the two extremes, and even if the very wealthy affected, out of coxcombry, Venetian goblets made from the brittle, thinly-blown soda-glass, there can be no doubt about the vast number of silver and silver-mounted vessels either used, or available for use, in Elizabethan England.

In regard to the source of at least part of the enormous quantities of silver used in the manufacture of drinking vessels, at a time when plate-ships were crossing the Atlantic fairly frequently from the New World to Spain, we may quote from a German writer,[1] who said of the English in 1598: 'they are good sailors, and better pirates'.

[1] Paul Hentzner.

CHAPTER THREE

EARLY STUART

1600–1660

IN THE early 17th century, certain medical authorities were of the opinion that the use of silver drinking vessels was beneficial for the health, and it is possible that this stimulated trade to some extent.

The Elizabethan style did not come to a sudden end on the death of Queen Elizabeth in 1603, but continued, with diminishing vigour, well into the reign of James I. The reaction against the German influence, which had been chiefly responsible for the richly ornamental character of much 16th-century silverware, became steadily stronger, and by the end of the first quarter of the 17th century a new, simpler style was firmly established.

Surface decoration did not entirely disappear from all classes of drinking vessels, but when embossing was resorted to, it was executed in far lower relief, the degree of projection being so slight that the form of the object concerned remained unimpaired.

Very occasionally, an impressive standing cup, commissioned by some eminent body such as a Livery Company or a College, might display a certain outmoded lavishness of ornament, especially if it happened to be in some typically Germanic form, but the most high-esteemed type of cup in the first half of the 17th century was always decorated in a manner combining effectiveness with restraint.

STANDING CUPS

In the previous chapter, mention was made of a kind of standing cup with a bowl shaped like the more pointed half of an egg. These ovoid bowls were, for some years, the standard type used in connection with a new form of cup which appeared at the very end of the 16th century. Several surviving specimens bear the hall-mark for 1599, but as these are the very earliest of the species, and as the design was far more characteristic of the first half of the 17th century, it was decided to defer their consideration to the present chapter.

Most of them were provided with dome-shaped covers, and as these were surmounted by a triangular-section finial in the form of a hollow pyramid, these vessels are generally known by the modern descriptive term, 'Steeple Cups'. The pyramids were mostly in decorative open-work, but are occasionally found fashioned from sheet silver, often engraved with chevrons or other simple designs. They were usually supported on three minute scroll brackets at the angles.

The bowl illustrated in Fig. 38 is typical of the earlier representatives of the species, and the chief identification factor, the pyramid finial, is easily recognizable. The same feature sometimes occurred in Italy at the same period, but it cannot be assumed from this that it was anything but a native English design, particularly as it seems quite foreign to the Italian idiom, in which anything of a Gothic nature always appears strangely ill at ease.

Fig. 38. Bowl of steeple cup, early 17th century

The shape of the tall, ovoid bowl should be noted, because its presence generally indicates a date during the first decade of the 17th century. In Plate 11b is shown a cup with the type of blunter, round-funnel bowl which succeeded it.

Steeple cups were naturally no more immune from the loss of their covers than other forms of standing cup, but any specimen encountered may be readily identified and assigned to its period of origin on the evidence provided by other factors, which emerge from a study of Plate 11b.

Chief among these is the stem. Stems were subject to a certain degree of variation, but the vast majority consisted primarily of some kind of spherical, or nearly spherical knop, with smaller subsidiary mouldings above and below, forming together an elaborate inverted baluster, somewhat reminiscent of the legs of Dutch tables.

These knops, or potkins, were almost invariably connected with the topmost section of the stem, immediately below the bowl, by scroll brackets of varying degrees of elaboration, some of the most attractive and finely-finished being in the form of terminal monsters or female figures, the latter looking somewhat like ships' figureheads.

It will be observed that the stem itself is very short, and contemporary silversmiths seem to have realized that, in order to obviate any unpleasant disparity, and to establish a just proportion between the support of the vessel and the tall bowl with its cover and high finial, the foot would have to be modified in some way. This was achieved by extending it upward to give the impression that it was virtually part of the stem.

Most steeple cups were monumental objects for ceremonial use by several persons, rather than individual drinking vessels, and, as may be seen from the illustrations, they were very often decorated in some way to give them added importance.

The decoration is also in some degree indicative as to period, so that it is often possible to distinguish, by this means, cups made in the first ten years or so of the 17th century from those made later.

In general, the bowls of the earlier steeple cups tended to be decorated all over with a single repeating motif, which diminished progressively in size towards the base of the bowl. Probably the most popular of these motifs was the scallop shell, as in Fig. 38, but others were also used in the same manner, such as pears and bunches of grapes, the latter being sometimes interspersed with fruits of some other kind to fill up the intervals. These designs were usually repeated on the cover, though not necessarily on the foot, which might be embellished with long acanthus leaves, shallow gadroons, or other patterns.

Another type of bowl, more rarely encountered but belonging to the beginning of the century, was of hemispherical form, and was probably a survival from the Elizabethan period. The cover of such a cup was of the same shape as the bowl, so that the two together formed a complete sphere. The stem, foot, and pyramid finial were the same as on other examples, but when the cover is in position, there is a lack of balance between the parts due to the over-dominance of the bowl, and when it is missing, either through accident or intention, there is always an unresolved struggle for domination between the bowl and the foot, owing to insufficient boldness in the design of the stem.

Most of these cups were decorated in some way, but some, like an example at Trinity College, Cambridge, were entirely plain, apart from slight stamped ornament round the basal footring, though the scroll brackets on the stem add greatly to the interest of the general outline.

From about the middle of the reign of James I, the blunt round-funnel bowl became the standard type on steeple cups, and the decoration generally ceased to be of the all-over variety. Sometimes the bowl was divided into two unequal zones by a horizontal moulding at the top of the lower third, and the ornament in the two parts was usually of a different kind, that at the base being most frequently in the form of acanthus leaves.

Even when the moulding was absent, the division in the surface of the bowl was generally maintained by the decoration, and by the end of the first quarter of the century a type had appeared with a calix of embossed leafage at the base, and the area above it plain, apart from some perfunctory engraving or flat chasing. This is an indication of the increasing tendency towards plainness of surface in all branches of silversmiths' work.

The pyramid finial was extremely popular in the first half of the 17th century, and appeared, not only on other types of cup with bowls of unorthodox shape, such as the gourd-shaped bowls which were first popularized in England in the 16th century, but also on other objects such as the covers of salt-cellars.

Though the total height of steeple cups tended to be comparatively great, owing to the formation of the bowl and the tall finial, the bowls were usually of fairly reasonable size, especially when it is remembered that they were mostly used on ceremonial occasions, when a number of persons pledged each other in turn from the same vessel, but very occasionally they were immense.

A steeple cup presented to the borough of St. Ives, Cornwall, in 1640, was no less than 33 inches high, although by this time, the popularity of the type had very greatly diminished.

The traditional tendency to make silver-mounted standing cups of such materials as glass and coco-nuts continued up to the middle of the 17th century, after which vessels of this kind appeared more rarely. If they are cups of any importance they will have covers which are normally surmounted by a pyramid finial, so that their identification presents no great difficulty.

In addition to large, imposing standing cups like those which have already been considered, the fashion for small, individual wine cups, which had become popular in the 16th century, gained ground in the early 17th century, and persisted until they were almost entirely ousted by drinking glasses after the Restoration.

One of the first types to appear after 1600 had a shallow bowl, either hemispherical or saucer-like, a narrow stem consisting chiefly of an inverted baluster, and a low, conical foot like that of a wineglass. An example is illustrated in Plate 12a, and it will be seen that identification is a simple matter.

The bowls of these cups were very often decorated all over by embossing from the outside in the form of tiny pyramidal projections in close contact with each other. On the inside of the bowl, these projections appeared somewhat like the relief diamonds which were such a popular feature of early 19th-century glass-cutting, and no doubt improved the appearance of the wine by reflecting light through it, after the fashion of a wine-taster.

Other wine cups of similar size had stems and feet of much the same kind, but different bowls. At the beginning of the century a miniature form of the ovoid bowl was in use, but with rather straighter sides, as in Fig. 39. This was soon succeeded, as in the case of steeple cups, by a round-funnel bowl with blunt base. As the century advanced, stems tended to become taller and more slender either actually, or in relation to their height.

Fig. 39. Bowl of wine cup, early 17th century

Decoration was usually of a modest nature, and towards the end of the reign of James I, practically died out altogether. Richness of effect was reserved for the more important-looking large standing cups. In the first decade of the century, designs consisted mostly of versions of the floral and foliate scrolls popular at the end of the 16th century, and the background of the design was often matted to give an effect of relief without any actual projection.

In addition to bowls of normal circular section, some were polygonal, mostly with eight sides, and the panels thus formed were usually chased with a conventionalized plant motif against a matted background. The lower part often bore a leaf design embossed in very low relief and defined by chasing.

All these wine cups with slender baluster stems represent a continuance of the late Elizabethan tradition. This began to lose the remainder of its force early in the reign of Charles I, and in the 1630s, a type of cup of totally different character appeared.

It was distinguished by the sort of robustness of proportion which had characterized Elizabethan vessels such as Sir Nicholas Bacon's cup (Plate 9b), and displayed also a stem consisting substantially of a stout inverted baluster, but the bowl, instead of being a modified hemisphere or an ovoid, was shaped like a bucket, and the vessel as a whole was more simply conceived, and totally devoid of surface decoration.

A typical example is shown in Plate 12b. The average height of these cups was about 7 inches, and it is evident from the fact that they were sometimes made in sets—some of which have survived—that they were intended as individual drinking vessels.

They all display a strong family likeness, in spite of minor variations in the proportions of the several elements composing the stems, and familiarity with one example is sufficient to make their identification a simple matter. They cannot be confused with cups of the preceding century if the shape of the bowls is borne in mind, and the lack of decorative elaboration on the stems.

Fig. 40. Small cup with trumpet stem, mid-17th century

In Fig. 40 is shown a more meanly-designed cup of a type which appeared in the first half of the century, and persisted into the Commonwealth and slightly beyond. All these cups had the same sort of trumpet stem, accompanied by a round-funnel or bucket-shaped bowl. These elements varied somewhat in proportion, but the whole vessel was seldom more than 4 or 5 inches high.

Some were entirely plain, others bore some rather poor chasing or engraving, as in the example illustrated. They occasionally found their way into churches for use as communion cups, and were apparently considered more suitable for liturgical use than the beautiful mediaeval chalices destroyed in the previous century.

BEAKERS

The enduring popularity of the modest beaker was probably due to a number of reasons. Since it was an essentially simple vessel, it was no doubt cheaper than a standing cup or a tankard, as it lacked the stem and foot of the first, and the handle and lid of the second. It was also very stable, and one of average capacity was useful for containing a variety of beverages. They were made in several sizes, from large stoups which contained a generous measure of ale, to small beakers for children, but those of medium height seem to have been most popular.

The beakers of the early 17th century were identical with those of the second half of the preceding century, but as time went on, an increasing number were made without any decoration at all, and some of them widened rather more towards the rim, and had smaller feet.

The small-scale, repeating-die ornament round the foot-ring, which had been almost invariable in the Elizabethan period, tended to disappear as the century advanced, and to be replaced by simple mouldings, but there was no great change in their appearance until the Restoration, and even then, the differences were more a matter of ornament than of basic form.

TANKARDS

English beer in the early 17th century seems to have enjoyed something of an international reputation. Fynes Moryson, writing in 1617, said: 'The English beer is famous in Netherland

and lower Germany, which is made of barley and hops. . . . The cities of lower Germany upon the sea forbid the public selling of English beer, to satisfy their own brewers, yet privately swallow it like nectar. But in Netherland great and incredible quantity thereof is spent.'

If it was appreciated in north-western Europe, it was vastly popular in its country of origin, and an increasing number of silver tankards were made to contain it, many of them no doubt taking the place of the now outmoded silver-mounted tankards of Rhenish stoneware whose owners had come up in the world.

As with other kinds of silverware, the decorated Elizabethan types continued for some time into the reign of James I, but by 1625, the great majority of tankards were more or less plain, and gilding had become an exception.

Fig. 41. Cylindrical tankard, about 1620

The most popular variety seems to have been of almost true cylinder form, with a lid like a flattened dome with bulging, rounded edges, as in Fig. 41. In the post-Reformation mania for simplicity in ecclesiastical plate, numbers of these tankards were acquired by churches for use as communion flagons, a circumstance to which many of them probably owe their preservation.

If the example illustrated is compared with the 16th-century specimen in Fig. 34, it will be noticed that the former is shorter, and wider in diameter, marking the inception of a tendency that was to continue far into the second half of the 17th century when it reached its peak.

No doubt this change in proportion was partly due to the decline of German influence, but it may also be attributable in some degree to the fact that a shorter, wider vessel could be knocked over far less easily than one with a high centre of gravity.

Larger versions of these tankards were designed as serving vessels, and Mr. Charles Oman has pointed out that it was in about 1625 that they began to be known as 'flagons' instead of livery pots.[1]

Early in the reign of Charles I, an even squatter form of tankard began to be made, and can be identified by the absence of a foot-ring, as with certain contemporary pewter pots, a flat lid made of a single piece of sheet plate, extending into a point opposite the handle, and an entirely new form of thumb-piece consisting of an upward-curving ramp surmounted by a horizontal cylinder of varying length and thickness.

These tankards continued into the Civil War period. An example is shown in Fig. 42 displaying all the features mentioned above.

Though the absence of the foot-ring from the tankards in question no doubt saved the silversmith a certain amount of trouble, it was undesirable from a practical standpoint, as it meant that the base of the actual receptacle was in direct contact with the table or other surface, and was accordingly liable to become dented, or even perforated.

This disadvantage was obviated in another design which was produced before the outbreak of the Civil War, and remained popular until slightly after the return of Charles II in 1660. The new type was provided with a comparatively high foot-ring,

[1] *English Church Plate*, 1957.

Fig. 42. Tankard without foot-ring, Charles I

Fig. 43. Mid-17th century tankard with skirt-base

spreading far beyond the sides, and with a decidedly concave profile, usually described nowadays as a 'skirt-base'. No more stable vessel of the same species has ever existed.

At the same time, some modification occurred in the form of the lid. It was probably discovered that a tankard without any headroom under the cover caused the foam from a good measure of beer to escape under the edge of the lid and run down the sides of the body. This was dealt with by making the lid in the form of a low, flat-topped dome, and these are known to collectors as 'single-step covers'.

All the identification factors mentioned may be seen in the tankard illustrated in Fig. 43. A fair number have survived, and they turn up in the saleroom from time to time. An example of 1641 belongs to the church of Freefolk, Hampshire, and another, made in 1653, is in the possession of the Carpenters Company.

According to the author's observations, the period of the greatest incidence of these vessels was the ten years from 1650 to 1660, and many specimens, dating from this time, are raised from metal of somewhat thin gauge, due no doubt to the political uncertainty and economic stringency which prevailed during the Commonwealth, which had a damping effect on silversmithing activities in general.

Towards the end of the Commonwealth period, a form of tankard began to be produced in certain provincial centres which was totally at variance with all English traditions of silversmithing. It is considered to have originated in Scandinavia, and all surviving examples, which are somewhat rare, have been found to bear the marks of the Edinburgh, York, Newcastle, or Hull assay offices. They are more characteristic of the post-Restoration period, and will therefore be considered in the next chapter.

Although silver-mounted earthenware pots were hardly ever made after 1600, tankards of marble, particularly the sort known as 'serpentine', continued to enjoy a modest degree of popularity.

They may be identified as belonging to the various parts of the 17th century by the style of the silver mounts, as these correspond to the similar features of tankards made entirely of silver. In the first quarter of the century, for example, lids were usually domed, and with a finial at the apex, while an example in the Victoria and Albert Museum, made in the late 1630s, has a lid made of a flat disc of silver, and a thumb-piece of the type already illustrated in Fig. 42.

In addition to the lid, other parts in silver were a foot-ring, a handle, a lip-band, and a band encircling the body just below the centre. These bands were essential for the attachment of the handle, which could naturally not be soldered to the marble.

Coco-nut shells were occasionally used to form the bodies of English silver-mounted tankards, though they were very seldom made, and the reader is unlikely to encounter one, but an ostrich-egg has been employed for this purpose in a tankard in the British Museum. It is provided with silver-gilt mounts of fine quality, with the date-letter for 1609, but like a coco-nut tankard, it consists virtually of a covered standing cup with a handle, though the presence of this feature undoubtedly qualifies it for inclusion among the tankards.

Tankards of this kind occurred rather more frequently in Germany, often with a lower, or quite rudimentary stem, but they were exceedingly uncommmon in England, partly, perhaps on account of the fragility of the material, and the fact that the design displays a certain self-conscious refinement which appears unsuitable for a vessel to contain beer.

TWO-HANDLED CUPS

Popular nomenclature of doubtful validity so bedevils the subject of two-handled cups, that it is best to call all varieties by this simple name.

In the first half of the 17th century, three basic types were in use in England, though it is impossible to assert that they never existed before.

The first was tall in relation to its width, and varied between about 3 and 9 inches in height. Owing to its average capacity, it was almost certainly used for small beer. In shape, it displayed a certain affinity with the tall two-handled cup of 16th-century date already illustrated in Fig. 36, but with a more fluent profile of ogee form. It was probably more convenient to drink from than the earlier variety.

The body, hand-raised in one piece, stood upon a stout, spreading foot, which was usually narrower than the most protuberant part and somewhat wider than the rim, but the most easily recognizable feature, which was common to all these cups whenever they were made, was the two small, circular handles soldered to opposite sides of the neck, and looking somewhat like a pair of spectacles. The earliest specimen extant was made in 1616, and is in the possession of the Mercers Company of the City of London. An example may be seen in Fig. 44.

Fig. 44. 'College cup', early 17th century

These vessels are generally known as 'College Cups', owing to the fact that a number are known to have been in use at Cambridge University before the Civil War, and some are still preserved in various Oxford colleges and at Eton, but it seems almost certain that their use was not confined to institutions of this kind.

Some of them contained a good deal of silver, and those in the possession of other bodies and private individuals would have been more vulnerable to sequestration during the Civil War, when enormous quantities of plate were seized by one side or the other, and converted into coin to pay the troops.

Related to the foregoing, but of different proportions, was another type of two-handled cup of which examples still survive from the reign of Charles I. This preserved the ogee-shaped

11a. Elizabethan silver-mounted stoneware tankard. *Height:* $6\frac{1}{8}''$
(*Victoria and Albert Museum*)

11b. James I steeple cup. *Height:* $17\frac{1}{8}''$
(*Victoria and Albert Museum*)

12a. Shallow wine cup, 1603. *Height:* 5″
(*British Museum*)

12b. Charles I wine cup with bucket bowl.
Height: $6\frac{5}{8}$″
(*Victoria and Albert Museum*)

body, but was shorter and of more squat appearance, had handles of a completely different kind, and was usually provided with a cover. Cups of essentially the same type, in varying sizes, were to be immensely popular in the Charles II period.

The handles were of two main kinds, and consisted either of simple, recurved scrolls, cast in the solid, or scrolls of a more decorative kind embodying terminal female figures, of varying degrees of nudity. The latter appear to be basically a larger version of the smaller scrolls of various kinds which so frequently embellished the potkins of steeple cups, as mentioned earlier in this chapter.

The bodies, which were supported on a low foot, were normally of circular section, but an example of 1649, formerly in the collection of Lord Swaythling, was twelve-sided, the flat facets continuing out to the edge of the foot-ring, and over the cover from flange to finial.

This form of treatment was uncommon in the 17th century, but was re-popularized on other kinds of hollowware by immigrant Huguenot silversmiths in the early 18th century. Fig. 45 shows a short, ogee-shaped cup possessing all the usual features.

Fig. 45. Charles I two-handled cup

Vessels of this kind are generally described, without any certainty of correctness, as 'Caudle Cups' or 'Posset Cups'. Caudle and posset were hot, viscous beverages or semi-liquid foods, consisting of milk soured with spiced wine or ale, or thin gruel mixed with the same liquors, but although the two-handled cups in question were, in fact, probably used to contain these unpleasant-sounding concoctions, it is highly improbable that the owner of one would have felt in any way restrained from using it for other things such as mulled ale or hippocras, or even for ordinary beer or wine.

It is sometimes suggested that the presence of a cover must indicate contents that had to be kept hot, such as caudle or posset, but in view of the long history of covered cups of various kinds, it seems unnecessary to go so far to account for the feature in question.

The third type bore a general similarity to the mediaeval cup preserved in the Treasury of St. Mark's, Venice, considered in the last chapter. The body had straight sides, sloping outward to the lip and often slightly everted, a low foot, and scroll handles of the various types current at the period, including those already discussed, with female terminal figures.

There was nothing especially graceful about the shape of these cups, and the meanly-conceived ornament, sometimes applied during the Commonwealth, did little to improve their appearance. The example shown in Plate 13a is entirely typical both in form and decoration.

They were made in a large range of sizes, and a great many were never equipped with covers. The workmanship was occasionally very poor, and the silver extremely thin, though this may well have been due to a desire to accommodate those with ill-lined pockets, during the joyless days of the Puritan ascendancy.

It is to cups of this kind, including those of later periods, that the unfortunate term 'porringer' has been applied, though their unlikely connection with porridge has never been established.

There had always been a tendency for people to attempt, as a matter of priority, to provide themselves with drinking vessels of silver, while remaining content to eat their food from pewter, earthenware, or treen, and one would have supposed that they would be even more likely to be satisfied with food-vessels of a humble nature at a time of economic stress.

Furthermore, while the existence of silver porringers in the 16th and 17th centuries is well attested by contemporary documents, Shakespeare, in *The Taming of the Shrew*, makes Petruchio say to his haberdasher, who has offered him a cap, 'Why, this was moulded on a porringer, A velvet dish,' and it seems unreasonable that a deep, two-handled cup of the type under discussion, should be described as a dish.

At the period with which we are concerned, there existed large numbers of pewter vessels of variable width, but invariable shallowness, with a flat lug, or handle, projecting horizontally from the rim. A few were made in silver, and an example is illustrated in the next chapter. These shallow vessels are sometimes found doing duty as the covers of skillets, and other cooking-pots, which establishes their connection with solid food. It is assuredly this type of vessel which is your true porringer, and it is interesting to note that the term is always used in this connection in the United States, where old English usages often persist long after they have been discarded in England itself.

While the college cup is of importance because the shorter cup of the same shape may well have developed from it, the two smaller vessels existed in greater numbers, and spawned a numerous progeny which continued into the 18th century.

Other two-handled cups of rarer type existed at the same time as those mentioned above, and will be briefly considered.

The identification of the first presents no difficulty if the appearance of the tankard with skirt-base is remembered. This cup was of precisely the same form and proportions, only in place of the single S-shaped handle of hollow sheet silver, it had the usual pair of handles in cast scroll-work, and the single-step cover, instead of being hinged, was of the normal loose variety, with some kind of simple finial in the centre to enable it to be removed.

Another uncommon type had a wide, hemispherical bowl raised on a trumpet-shaped stem, and with handles of the usual kind. An attractive specimen in the Victoria and Albert Museum has a body made of mother-of-pearl, built up from vertical flat strips in a manner suggestive of coopering. The mounts are of silver, and the lip-band and stem are connected by the usual straps.

No mention has been made in this chapter of a Commonwealth style, because, in fact, no such style really existed. Plate had already become simpler before Cromwell's military dictatorship commenced, and followed a normal line of development largely unconnected with the Puritans' notorious hatred of beauty.

Dutch influence was beginning to make itself felt before the Restoration, but as the style of decoration which this influence produced was more typical of the reign of Charles II, it will be dealt with in the next chapter.

CHAPTER FOUR

LATE STUART

1660–1700

ALTHOUGH CHARLES II made lavish gifts of plate to his mistresses, the phenomenal increase in production which followed the restoration of the monarchy in 1660 had little to do with the profligate morals and spendthrift extravagance of the Court. The whole country had become heartily sick of sour-faced, theocratic government, and joy and relief may have provided some psychological stimulus, but it seems evident that the chief cause of the upsurge of silversmithing activity was a general desire to replace the huge quantities of plate which had been melted down during the Civil War, to fill the war-chests of King or Parliament.

Those who had shared the King's long exile in Europe had become acquainted with a more luxurious style of living, and after their return, the demand for silversmiths' work extended over a much wider range. This involved the manufacture of silver objects which had been unknown before the Commonwealth, but did not involve any increase in types of drinking vessels. On the contrary, what had been the most important type of all almost ceased to have any functional significance.

This was the standing cup. Covered standing cups of imposing aspect continued to be made, though on a more modest scale, but these were required by official bodies of various kinds rather than by private individuals.

The small wine cup practically disappeared altogether, its

place in fashionable esteem having been usurped by the two-handled cup, and the drinking glass both imported and domestic, the latter adding insult to injury by appropriating the inverted baluster stem, especially after the invention of lead-glass by George Ravenscroft.

STANDING CUPS

The bucket-shaped bowl, introduced in the reign of King Charles I, continued, in various guises, to be the most widely-used form of receptacle for standing cups, but the stem, foot, and cover were modified.

The type of steeple cup which dominated the first half of the century had become obsolete, but stylistic details are so tenacious of life that a degenerate form of the steeple still persisted on the covers of many ceremonial cups.

These pyramids were constructed in a totally different manner from their predecessors, and instead of being made separately, and supported on small scroll brackets, were drawn by the hammer of the craftsman from the metal of the cover itself, and were of circular, instead of triangular section.

Fig. 46. Late form of steeple cover, Charles II

Fig. 47. Typical stem of Charles II standing cup

A typical steeple-shaped cover of the Charles II period is shown in Fig. 46. These modified pyramids were mostly surmounted by either a turned vase-shaped finial, or by a small cast figure of some kind. They became less common later in the century, when the pyramid was often replaced by a bold inverted baluster standing on a spool-shaped collet, or a cast figure supported in the same manner.

The tall trumpet foot with rounded top, which was usual in the first half of the century, disappeared quickly, its place being taken by a very short trumpet beneath an annular moulding, or a flattened dome with the stem rising from the centre. Feet of these kinds will be seen later in the illustrations.

The chief distinction was in the form of the stem, the most popular kind apparently providing the inspiration for Newcastle glass-makers in the following century. It may be identified by its greatly increased height apart from the foot, and the general occurrence of an inverted baluster, helped out by a varying number of mouldings above and below. The scroll brackets, which had been an almost invariable feature of the earlier stems, had quite disappeared (Fig. 47).

More rarely, the subsidiary mouldings were dispensed with, and to provide the necessary height, the inverted baluster was made very much larger, the most protruberant part bulging in a very decided manner. A similar feature occurred on the stems of contemporary Dutch brass candlesticks, which were imported into England in large numbers.

The base of the baluster usually stood on a single bold protuberance, which was either supported on a short trumpet-shaped process, merging into the rest of the foot, or formed a separate entity altogether, and was fixed to the centre of a foot of flattened dome shape. The elaborately decorated standing cup presented by Samuel Pepys to the Clothworkers' Company shortly after the Restoration had a stem of this kind.

Figs. 48, 49, and 50 show three typical vessels of the reign of Charles II.

The bowls were treated in a variety of ways, being left quite plain, engraved with large floral and other motifs of Dutch origin, or embossed with all-over designs of a similar kind. In addition to decorative patterns, an annular moulding is sometimes found,

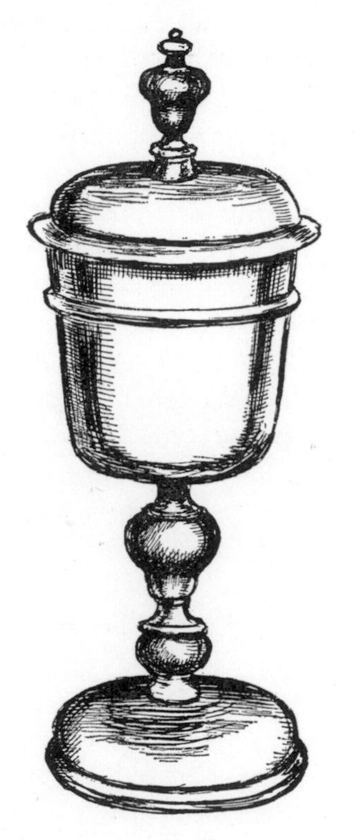

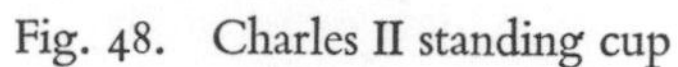

Fig. 48. Charles II standing cup

Fig. 49. Charles II standing cup

encircling the bowl a short distance below the rim, as in Figs. 48 and 50.

More rarely encountered is a strange decorative technique which involved the enclosing of the body of a vessel in a chased and pierced casing or sleeve, through which the gilded lower surface was visible. The designs used for the white silver sleeve were similar in character to those which often appeared in the form of embossing, and comprised rich masses of foliage or flowers, sometimes with animals or large birds such as turkeys. The standing cup presented by Pepys to the Cloth worker's Company was treated in this manner, but most surviving vessels in this style are in the form of two-handled cups, an example of which will be seen later.

Numerous forgeries and reproductions exist of a very uncommon type of late 17th-century vessel known as a Wager Cup, or Puzzle Cup.

One of the few genuine English examples still extant is in the possession of the Vintners' Company of London, and is fairly typical of the class as a whole, which is much better represented in Holland.

These vessels were all constructed according to the same principle. They consisted of a large bowl, which formed the foot when the cup was not in use, and to this was attached a formal or fanciful stem, which branched out into a pair of pivots. A smaller bowl was confined between these by minute trunnions,

Fig. 50. Charles II standing cup

Fig. 51. Wager cup, late 17th century

which enabled it to swing freely and remain level, in whatever position the cup was held.

In the Vintners' Company there is a tradition that every member was obliged to drink the health of the company from the large bowl, then reverse the cup and pledge the Master from the smaller vessel without spilling any liquor.

An example of one of these wager cups is shown in Fig. 51. The smaller bowl is slightly embossed with acanthus leaves: a form of decoration exceedingly popular in Holland, and which was found on many kinds of English hollowware at the same period.

A Dublin wager cup of 1706, in the Victoria and Albert Museum, is practically identical with the above, the chief differences being that the small bowl is undecorated, and the female figure wears a three-cornered hat.

Wager cups came into brief vogue once more during the 1820s, when there was a tendency to hark back to the styles of previous periods; they were often of archaic form, but the hallmarks remove all doubt as to their period of origin. Still later specimens are often unmarked, and are probably deliberate forgeries. Collectors are recommended to ponder very deeply before deciding to acquire such an object.

BEAKERS

Beakers continued to be made after the Restoration, but were less popular than formerly, probably because their function was increasingly taken over by glasses. Most of them were of slightly different proportions from earlier examples, and tended to become shorter and wider like those of the Middle Ages.

Many were quite plain, as in Fig. 52, others had a narrow horizontal moulding a short distance below the rim, while some were embossed with the florid leafage and flowers which appeared on other types of silverware (Figs. 53 and 54).

In addition to these obviously functional vessels, many of which were only 4 or 5 inches high, others occasionally appeared whose large size and elaborate decoration introduce some doubt as to their real purpose.

Fig. 52. Plain Charles II beaker

Fig. 53. Embossed Charles II beaker

Fig. 54. Embossed Charles II beaker

An example of 1661 has been noted with a height of nearly 18 inches. This has a rim which is everted to such an extent that it projects horizontally, and another specimen at Welbeck Abbey is 14 inches high and is fitted with a cover. The fact that these gigantic beakers are commonly embossed with designs which are often found on large silver chimney-piece vases, suggests that they were intended to be decorative, rather than useful, and were quite possibly meant to stand on chimney-pieces themselves.

Another type of less formal drinking vessel became increasingly popular in the late 17th century, though it is not known precisely when it first came into use. This was the silver Tumbler, known also as a Tumbler-cup or Tumbling Bowl. The last-named was mentioned as early as the reign of Charles I, and the use of the word 'bowl' suggests that it was a somewhat wide, shallow vessel.

Most surviving members of the species are of this type, or related in form to the beaker.

The most important characteristic common to all these vessels is the rounded base, which was considerably thicker and heavier than the sides, the greater weight of the part concerned causing the tumbler to resume an upright position after being rocked about or knocked. The temptation to children to do this deliberately must sometimes have been irresistible.

The name clearly derives from the tendency to sway from side to side, a fact which demonstrates the unsuitability of the term when applied to a very stable form of modern drinking glass of the beaker variety.

It seems that tumblers were originally intended for use while travelling, as part of canteens, which might be frequently called into service during long coach journeys. They were made in a range of sizes which suggests that some were designed for wine or spirits, and others for beer. They continued to be produced in the 18th century, particularly the smaller varieties, but they are devoid of artistic interest, nor is it easy to assign them to their period without reference to the hall-marks, unless they bear

Fig. 55. Tumbler cup

some form of decoration, which they seldom do. An example is shown in Fig. 55.

Dutch influence had been predominant in England through much of the 17th century, but strangely enough, when William of Orange and Mary, daughter of James II, were offered the crown by Parliament in February 1689, favourable conditions were created for this influence to be replaced by that emanating from the France of Louis XIV.

In spite of the hostilities between France and the Low Countries, French artistic influence was gradually spreading throughout the whole of western Europe, and it may be recalled that it was probably the Frenchman, Daniel Marot, brought to England in the train of the Stadtholder, who introduced the cabriole leg to English chair-makers.

The tendency was also reinforced, indirectly, by Louis XIV himself. In 1598, Henry IV had ensured religious freedom for all French citizens by the Edict of Nantes. In 1685, Louis XIV, possibly with some idea of currying favour with the Pope, revoked the Edict, though his Holiness, and many prominent Catholic clerics, strongly objected to the move.

Placed outside the protection of the law by the King's act, the unfortunate Huguenots were subjected to an intolerable persecution, which included the compulsory quartering of dragoons, who supported the King's political piety by pillage, rape, and murder. Great numbers of Huguenots left France and sought refuge in neighbouring Protestant countries, including Holland.

England could do little to relieve them while James II still reigned, but after the accession of William, many more of these Huguenots found refuge in England and Ireland. They included large numbers of silversmiths, and although their activities were at first resented by the English craftsmen, the styles of the two nationalities eventually fused, and produced very pleasing results in the first half of the 18th century.

One of the design-elements popularized, but not invented, by the immigrant Huguenots was gadrooning, though native silversmiths tended to use it in a different manner. They most commonly employed it in an elongated vertical or spiral form, which not only decorated, but also strengthened the somewhat thin walls of their vessels.

The Huguenots generally excluded it from the bodies of cups

altogether, and confined it to narrow, crowded bands on or adjacent to borders.

The humble beaker was often embellished with the English variant in the last decade of the 17th century, the long gadroons, alternating with concave flutes, being usually restricted to the lower part of the vessel, and supported artistically by a cabled moulding round the upper part. This may be seen in Fig. 56.

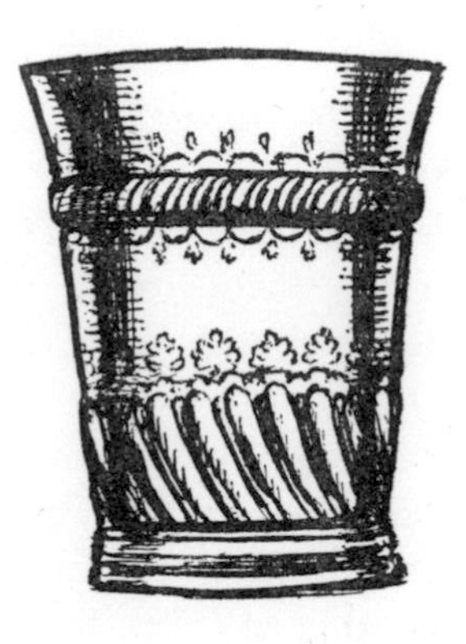

Fig. 56. Gadrooned beaker, late 17th century

Beakers of this kind continued to be made in the reign of Queen Anne, although by this time they had ceased to be of any significance as fashionable drinking vessels.

TANKARDS

While enormous quantities of claret were drunk in the second half of the 17th century in addition to English beer, devotees of the latter often made it their constant tipple to the exclusion of all else.

This is evident from the words of a contemporary lyric: 'Of honest malt liquor let English boys sing; A pox take French claret, we'll drink no such thing.'

Wine and strong ale, which was as potent as wine, were drunk from glasses, but the vessels used for small beer were lidless mugs of stoneware, pewter, and jacked leather, and tankards of pewter and silver, production of the last increasing enormously in the reigns of Charles II, James II, and William and Mary.

Elizabethan silver tankards, and those of the middle decades of the 17th century with skirt-bases, had mostly a capacity of one pint or thereabouts, but the opening words of another song of the period under discussion hint at a change which took place after the Restoration: 'Jack, thou'rt a toper, let's have t'other quart.'

The 'quart' referred to was drunk from one tankard, at a time when swindging thirsts were quenched from swindging vessels. A silver tankard of 1677, formerly in the author's collection, had a capacity of no less than three pints.

The increase in size necessitated by the increase in appetite brought about a change in proportion, and tankards became very much wider in relation to their height, tapering slightly from base to lip.

Fig. 57. Charles II tankard with single-step lid

The added stability resulting from this modification rendered the skirt-base of the earlier type unnecessary, and it rapidly became obsolete except on tall flagons, its place being taken by simple mouldings, of varying height, encircling the base and forming a foot-ring.

Several points should be noted to assist in identification. Until about 1675, lids remained of the single-step variety, the horizontal flange extending in one or several points opposite the handle. Foot-rings tended to be low, raising the base of the vessel only slightly above the level of the table. Thumb-pieces were mostly of simple form, one of the commonest spreading out into two identical lobes, like those already in use with tankards with skirt-bases. The lid was attached to the handle by a butt-hinge of five cylinders instead of the previous three.

Fig. 57 shows a typical tankard of the Restoration period. The top of the lid was either flat, or very slightly domed, the latter feature raising the suspicion in the minds of some collectors that such lids have been tampered with at a later date.

It would seem unlikely, however, from the very large number which have survived in this form, that they have been interfered with in any way, and there is no evidence to support the notion that tankard lids of the period were invariably flat-topped when they left the silversmith's hands.

In the second half of Charles II's reign, various slight changes began to appear. Although single-step lids continued to be made, double-step lids were far more numerous. The sides of the latter, above the flange, were of convex profile, and were surmounted by a very low step with vertical sides, as in Fig. 58.

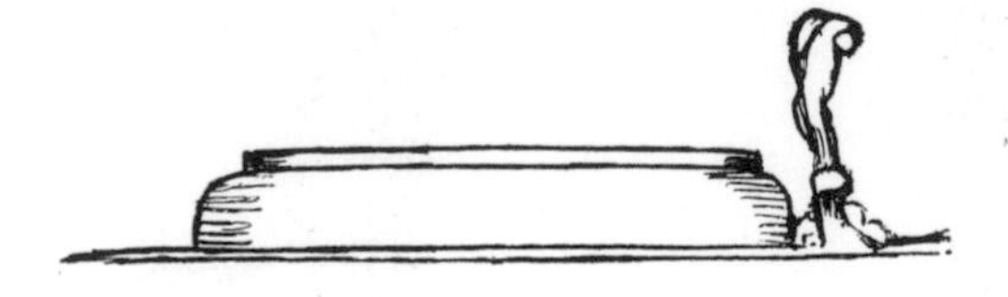

Fig. 58. Double-step tankard-lid

The flange of such a lid usually projected in several points, the central one being more prominent than the others.

The gauge of plate commonly employed after about 1678 was somewhat thinner than formerly, and it would seem that silversmiths were sometimes in doubt as to the ability of the metal

13a. Two-handled cup, mid-17th century. *Height:* $3\frac{1}{2}''$
(Victoria and Albert Museum)

13b. Charles II tankard. *Height:* $6\frac{1}{2}''$
(Victoria and Albert Museum)

14. York tankard of Scandinavian type. *Height:* $7\frac{1}{4}''$
(Victoria and Albert Museum)

to withstand distortion when the weight of an already heavy vessel was increased by a full measure of beer.

They dealt with the matter by modifying the form of the handle, which threw out a spur, extending vertically down the back of the tankard and soldered to the body. This may be seen in Fig. 59.

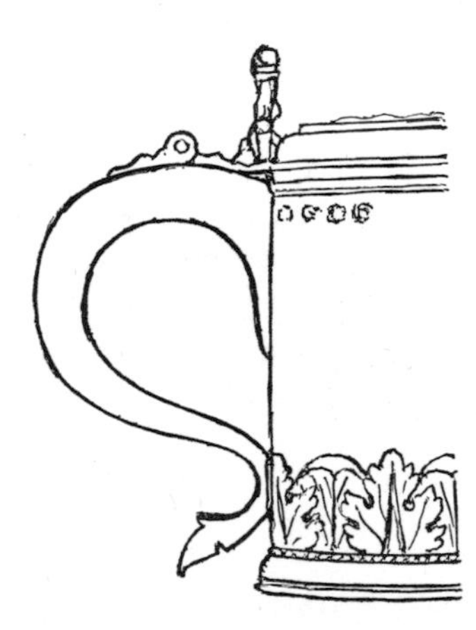

Fig. 59. Tankard-handle with spur

By means of this device, the rigidity of the vessel was much enhanced, and the body was sometimes still further strengthened by a narrow annular moulding, encircling it at any point between the middle and a short distance above the base.

Plain tankards were popular throughout the period, but many others were decorated in various ways. The type of decoration most frequently used consisted of a circuit of embossed acanthus and other leaves, spreading upward from the base immediately above the foot-ring, and terminating below the middle. These bands of formalized leaves varied in height from one tankard to another (Fig. 59).

The remaining surface was usually left plain, but very occasionally some low-relief floral ornament is found on the upper part of the body. On these decorated tankards, the handle-spur, shown in Fig. 59, which formed a long triangle at its junction with the body of the vessel, was sometimes surrounded and emphasized by a lightly chased acanthus leaf, in which the spur took the place of the central leaf-rib.

The lid of a tankard ornamented in the above manner might be one of three main kinds: entirely plain, embossed from the under-side with curving acanthus foliage swirling outwards from the middle, or with straight leaves radiating from the centre like broad spokes of a wheel, the last being the least common of all.

The hall-marks were struck, not only on the body, either underneath or immediately to the right of the handle, but also on the lid. It is evident from the frequent distortion of these marks, that silversmiths must often have submitted tankard lids for assay and marking in plain condition, and decorated them afterwards. The Wardens of the various assay offices were notoriously in-different to the presence of ornament on plate, and even if a silversmith had gone to a great deal of trouble in the way of embossing and chasing, the Warden would have struck the hall-marks in the customary place, without caring in the least whether it impaired the decoration or not.

The marks were applied by means of dies, which were held against the silver and given a heavy blow with a hammer, while the other side of the vessel was pressed against an anvil. This compressed the metal so much that subsequent embossing was unable to obliterate the marks altogether, though they are sometimes difficult to find among the decoration.

Oriental styles of ornament, which had been made known to England chiefly by the Dutch and English East India companies, became extremely popular after the Restoration, particularly in the form of lacquered furniture. It was not long before attempts were made to reproduce it in England, and the silversmiths also became to some extent victims of the prevailing vogue.

The form of the resulting decoration applied to silverware is generally known as 'chinoiserie', though there was nothing especially Chinese about it, but merely a vague pseudo-oriental-ism. It appeared in the form of linear chasing on tankards and other vessels, and consisted chiefly of exotic trees, large flam-boyant birds, and curious theatrical 'Chinamen', who give the impression of having travelled much in India.

The bodies of tankards treated in this manner were entirely covered with the decoration, an example of which is shown in Fig. 60. It had a certain naïve charm, and interfered in no way with the form of the tankard, but appears a little unsuitable for a vessel to contain beer. It persisted until the end of the century, declining in incidence with the passage of time.

Fig. 60. Example of Chinoiserie ornament

At the same time, thumb-pieces became more elaborate, and were made of heavy cast silver in such forms as entwined dolphins, foliage, and strapwork, though the simpler types continued to be used also.

Towards the end of Charles II's reign, thumb-pieces were sometimes cast in the form of a lion couchant lying comfortably across the back of the lid facing the front. On Scottish tankards, the forepaws occasionally rested on a ball. These lion thumb-pieces were more popular in the early 18th century.

A tankard of 1684, illustrated in Plate 13b, has a double-step lid, lion thumb-piece, and body chased with chinoiserie decoration.

The lid of a tankard of the period is unfortunately sometimes marred by careless workmanship, the area between the base of the thumb-piece and the rise of the lid being filled with a large quantity of lumpy silver-solder. A similar perfunctory style of finish is also frequently found at the point where the foot-ring is attached to the body, the solder often being in the form of small isolated blobs, owing to the failure of the silversmith to apply the moistened borax, which was used as a flux, in a continuous line.

Apart from the decorative effect produced by the simple mouldings, foot-rings were generally quite devoid of ornament, though a thin ornamental stringing was occasionally applied at the junction with the body. The author has noted a kind of decoration involving, not only chasing, but also piercing, as on a certain type of contemporary French chalice, but foot-rings of this sort were extremely rare in England, and are unlikely to be encountered.

Handles were very seldom decorated in any way, though examples with the extending spur were occasionally pierced on the underside, near the upper junction with the body, with a few small motifs such as petals, or heart-shaped perforations.

They were sometimes very poorly finished, and specimens have been noted with the inside of the handles covered with coarse, oblique file marks, which the silversmith had not troubled to remove. It seems remarkable that customers should have been prepared to accept them in this state.

In addition to the body and lid, handles were sometimes marked also, but only with the maker's mark. This is found on the outer side, usually below the main curve, and it is evident that it must have been struck on this strip of flat plate before the handle was assembled, as the die would otherwise have made an unsightly dent, leaving the mark without definition.

This is obviously the reason why many perfectly genuine handles were not marked at all: it would be a simple mistake for the craftsman to forget about the mark until the handle was soldered together, and by that time it would be too late.

A tankard is sometimes found to have a different maker's mark on the handle from that on the lid and body, but this is no reflection on its authenticity. Evidence as to co-operation between different craftsmen continues to accumulate, and it is easy to understand that if a silversmith had an urgent order for a tankard, he would not hesitate to acquire a ready-made handle from someone else. As for the customer, it would be a matter of complete indifference to him what marks appeared on various parts, providing the whole vessel was manifestly of sterling silver.

In the last chapter, brief mention was made of a type of silver tankard which originated in Scandinavia, and was introduced into northern England and Scotland shortly before the Restoration. They continued to be made in the Scandinavian countries well into the 19th century, but their popularity in England ceased with the 17th century.

They were different in almost every way from other contemporary English tankards, and are very easily identified.

The body of such a tankard usually tapered less than other varieties, and was supported as a rule, not on a foot-ring, but on three hollow ball feet, deeply cross-hatched on the outer side, possibly to suggest an open pomegranate, and attached to the body by curling leafage (Fig. 61). These ball feet were placed

Fig. 61. Ball-foot of Scandinavian-type tankard

equidistantly, with one immediately beneath the handle, and the other two on each side of the front. In rare instances this arrangement was reversed, one ball being in the front, and the others on each side of the handle.

The lids were mostly of two kinds, and represented a return to an older form. They were usually without the horizontal flange which occurred on other English tankards, and consisted of simple, flattened domes with either rounded edges, or straight edges forming an angle with the top. When closed, they coincided more or less exactly with the moulding round the lip of the body.

Thumb-pieces were almost invariably in the form of two silver balls, slightly engraved to represent pomegranates, and the pivot of the hinge on which the lid turned had domed ends.

The standard type of handle was double-scrolled, as in Fig. 62, and generally terminated in a small escutcheon, but handles and terminals of this kind were found on other tankards at the same time and later.

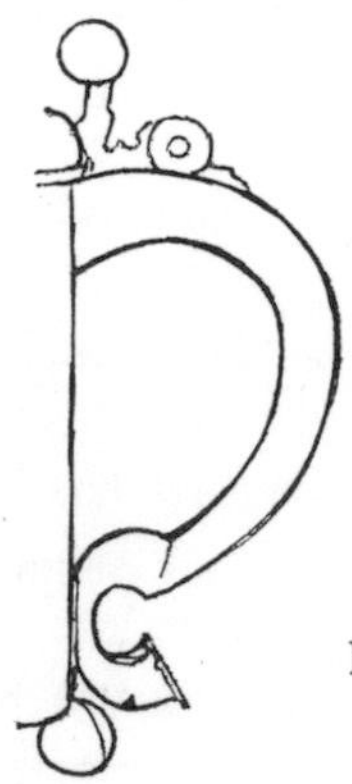

Fig. 62. Double-scroll tankard-handle

Plate 14 illustrates a fine York tankard of the above type, preserved in the Victoria and Albert Museum. It was made two or three years before the Restoration, but as explained earlier, vessels of this kind were far more typical of the two decades after 1660 than the Commonwealth period.

It will be observed that the example shown is decorated with large-scale floral engraving. This ornament is very Dutch in character, and occurred on other types of silverware as well, but the majority of these tankards were quite plain, apart, of course, from a coat of arms or crest, which is always liable to be found on the body opposite the handle. A Scottish example has been noted with heavily embossed ornament on the lower half of the body and the lid, but decoration of this kind was extremely uncommon.

Very occasionally, such a tankard is found with a normal foot-ring instead of the three ball feet. Specimens of this kind should always be examined with care to ensure that the foot-ring has not replaced ball feet which have been unsoldered at some time on account of damage.

There is no reason to suppose that some of them were not originally made with foot-rings, but the author once saw a gilded example with both a foot-ring, and three sets of leafage still in position above it. There was naturally no doubt as to what had happened in this case, but even if the leafage had not been present, gilding was entirely outmoded at the period in question, and can cover a multitude of sins.

These English tankards of Scandinavian type sometimes displayed a curious feature which is mentioned in the following quotation from Grose's *Classical Dictionary of the Vulgar Tongue*, published in the 18th century.

'Pin. In or to a merry pin; almost drunk: an allusion to a sort of tankard, formerly used in the north, having silver pegs or pins set at equal distances from the top to the bottom: by the rules of good fellowship, every person drinking out of one of these tankards, was to swallow the quantity contained between two pins; if he drank more or less, he was to continue drinking till he ended at a pin: by this means persons unaccustomed to measure their draughts were obliged to drink the whole tankard. Hence, when a person was a little elevated with liquor, he was said to have drunk to a merry pin.'

Students of 17th-century music may recall a contemporary song, not remarkable for its respectability, which begins: 'My Lady and her maid, upon a merry pin . . .'

Tankards of the above kind are usually known as 'peg tankards'. The pegs were generally soldered in a vertical line on the inside, opposite the handle, but are occasionally found fixed to the outside. They sometimes occurred also in tankards of the normal type current throughout the British Isles at the period in question.

A contemporary Newcastle tankard shown in Plate 15 is of composite character, displaying English and Scandinavian features together in the one vessel.

In the 17th century, a tankard was known in the language of thieves as a 'clank', a term which was obviously derived from the sound made by the lid. This noise was the cause of a great mischief to Sir James Shorter, Lord Mayor of London under James II in 1688. In August of that year, he set off to open

Bartholomew Fair, and reined-in his horse, as was the custom, to take a draught with the Keeper of Newgate. He was handed a tankard of spiced wine, but when he accidentally released the thumb-piece, the clank of the lid caused his horse to rear. Shorter was thrown on to his head, and died from his injuries a few days after.

Two interesting points may be gathered from this incident. In the first place, it is clear that our ancestors felt no compunction in using a tankard for liquors other than beer, and in the second place, we are reminded that the term 'tankard' is incorrect, when loosely applied in modern times to a similar vessel without a lid.

Lidless vessels of the tankard variety with a single handle are called Mugs, though smaller versions seem to have been known as 'cans'. They probably first began to appear in silver in the reign of Charles II.

They followed closely the form of similar vessels in pottery, and had bulbous bodies with cylindrical necks, somewhat like the Rhenish stoneware pots so often mounted in silver in the time of Queen Elizabeth, but very much smaller.

The necks of these silver mugs were usually embellished with numerous encircling lines. The handle of such a mug, comprising a flat ribbon of silver bent into the customary S-form, and chased with longitudinal parallel lines on the outer side, was of mean appearance and uncomfortable to hold. An example may be seen in Fig. 63.

Fig. 63. Charles II silver mug

These mugs continued to appear sparsely in the early 18th century, no doubt because they were cheaper to produce than others involving the use of more silver.

One sometimes comes across a lidless silver pot with Charles II hall-marks, and having the tapering cylindrical body and hollow, wrought handle characteristic of tankards. These pots are always of suspiciously generous capacity, and all those examined by the author have quite obviously been tankards that have lost their lids. They naturally fall under the general ban that applies to objects which are not in their original condition.

Silver drinking vessels in Scotland and Ireland bore a general similarity to those made in England at the same time, but a type of mug appeared in Scotland, late in the reign of Charles II, which does not appear to have been known south of the border.

This was called a Thistle-cup, but as it had a single handle, it may be regarded legitimately as a member of the mug family.

The vessel was mounted on a foot-ring, and the rounded base of the body was enclosed within a calix of vertical lobes. Above these was a moulded girdle with prominent central rib, and from this point, the sides flared strongly outward to the lip, giving the whole cup some resemblance to a thistle. The handle was of the usual scrolled form, cast in solid silver, sometimes with two projecting spurs, one on the outer side near the top, and the other on the inner side near the lower point of attachment to the body.

A thistle-cup is illustrated in Fig. 64. These attractive little mugs were made in various sizes, none of which was very large. Their capacity ranged from about half a pint to little more than that of a thimble, and as beer was never a very popular beverage in Scotland, and in any event, tankards were available for those who wanted it, it seems likely that the larger thistle-cups were used for claret, which was the Scottish national drink, and the smaller ones for spirits.

The earliest of these mugs so far noted was made in 1682, but the type had a very long life, and the author has seen a late 19th-century example, with a very slick, factory-made appearance, which was obviously intended as a christening mug.

No changes occurred in the styles of tankards or other drinking vessels in the short reign of James II, but under William and Mary, the last decade of the 17th century saw the popularization of new decorative techniques and the introduction of new features.

Fig. 64. Scottish thistle-cup

Some of these changes have already been alluded to in the section on beakers, earlier in this chapter, but tankards were susceptible of a wider range of treatment, on account of their size, and the greater number of component parts.

The same kind of gadrooning, alternating with concave flutes, appeared on the lower parts of tankards as on beakers, and was answered by a roped girdle encircling the upper section of the body.

More often than not, this girdle was interrupted in the front to accommodate the top of a large Baroque cartouche, enclosing an oval escutcheon for the owner's arms, crest, or monogram. The top and base of the cartouche consisted of acanthus foliage, reaching almost to the lip and base of the body, while the compartments at each side of the escutcheon were usually chased with a scale pattern. Above the basal gadroons, and on each side of the girdle, the transition from embossed to plain surfaces was often eased by small foliate motifs stamped with dies.

Sometimes, the cartouche was omitted altogether, and it must be admitted that the appearance of such a tankard, which already carried an adequacy of restless ornament, gained somewhat by the omission. The roped girdle, in this case, encircled the body completely, without interruption, and the arms, if any, were engraved on the plain surface beneath it.

Lids were treated in various ways, but if the body of the vessel was decorated with gadroons, these were almost invariably repeated on some part of the lid.

Plate 16a illustrates a late William III tankard of the type described above, and it will be noticed that the lid has developed a dome. This was by no means invariable in the late 17th century, but became a standard feature in the early part of the century following.

Gadrooning, which had been known in England at least since the late 15th century in one form or another, was used in the

Fig. 65. Tankard with gadrooned bands, late 17th century

Huguenot version to embellish candlesticks, ewers, and other silver objects, in which case it was mostly confined to narrow bands, which contrasted pleasantly with the neighbouring areas of plain metal.

The same technique was also applied to tankards, and Fig. 65 shows a late 17th-century example with the foot-ring and lid decorated in this restrained manner.

Apart from the ornament, it will be observed that the lid is surmounted by a finial, a feature which had been out of fashion since the early 17th century, but was now reintroduced on many tankards, and continued to appear during the reign of Queen Anne.

Although this feature was very occasionally found in the reign of Charles II, its wholesale reintroduction was almost certainly due to Huguenot influence. These French immigrants had come from a wine-producing country where beer-drinking was not a national habit, and tankards were probably quite unfamiliar to most of them. The finial and the decorative treatment no doubt represented an attempt to confer an important and monumental character on a vessel with whose basic design they felt little natural sympathy.

Both the tankards illustrated provide evidence of a subtle change of proportion which began to make itself felt in the late 17th century. Charles II tankards had been noticeably wide in relation to their height, but their width began to diminish under William III, and this process was continued in the 18th century, as will be seen later.

We must now consider an important type of decoration which came into occasional use shortly after the Restoration, but whose period of greatest incidence spanned the junction of the 17th and 18th centuries.

This is known as Cut-card work. Something very like it occurred on the goblet of 1545 shown in Fig. 25, but although it was found quite early in the reign of Charles II, and was not an invention of the Huguenot immigrants, they made more use of it than anyone else, and were no doubt responsible for making it popular.

It consisted of thin sheet silver, cut into various patterns mostly based on leaf-forms, soldered on to the body and sometimes the lid or cover of a vessel, and thus providing three-dimensional surface-interest without the necessity of embossing.

On tankards, it usually appeared round the base, immediately above the foot-ring, and sometimes on each side of a moulded girdle and on the lid. In Fig. 66 is shown a simple version of this decoration, which is very easily identified.

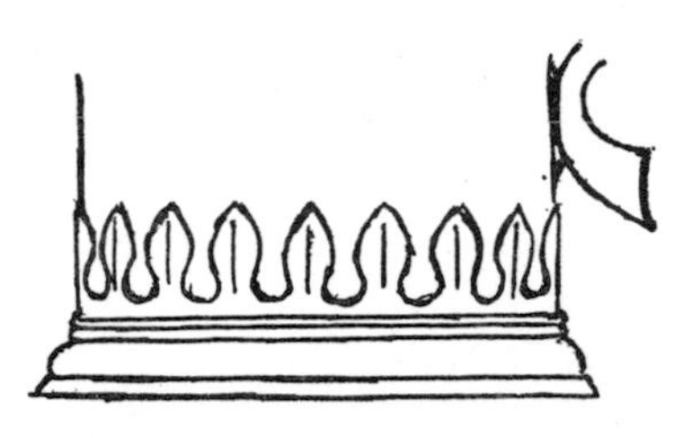

Fig. 66. Simple cut-card work

Rather more rarely, it surrounded the points of contact of the handle with the body, and was sometimes applied to the handle itself, usually in the form of an acanthus leaf. This was often further elaborated by a continuous row of diminishing silver beads which took the place of the usual leaf-rib.

Beading, of the kind referred to, was also used on handles by itself, and it is sometimes assumed that this form of decoration was not invented before the end of the 17th century. It occurs, however, on the handles of a pair of ornate flagons or tall tankards of 1646, in the possession of Thirkleby church in Yorkshire, though it would be true to say that it did not achieve any popularity until fifty years later.

In the last decade of the 17th century, England found herself in the grip of a serious financial crisis, to which many factors had contributed.

An entry in John Evelyn's diary for the 13th of July 1694 stated: 'Many executed at London for clipping money, now done to that intolerable extent, that there was hardly any money that was worth above half the nominal value.'

Nevertheless, the demand for plate continued undiminished, and as the coinage was of sterling quality, it seems likely that there was a flourishing business in coin-clippings, sold to the silversmiths to provide the raw material for their productions. There was no improvement in the situation by May 1696, for Evelyn wrote on the 13th of that month: 'Money still continuing exceeding scarce, so that none was paid or received, but all was on trust, the Mint not supplying for common necessities.'

It is clear that the acute shortage of money cannot be attributed entirely to the activities of the silversmiths, and Evelyn allotted some of the blame to the authorities in his entry for 3rd August 1696: 'The Bank lending the £200,000 to pay the army in Flanders, that had done nothing against the enemy, had so exhausted the treasure of the nation, that one could not have borrowed money under 14 or 15 per cent on bills, or on Exchequer tallies under 30 per cent.'

The government became alarmed at the damage suffered by the trade of the country, and made various attempts to deal with the situation, but these were frustrated by the national mania for plate-collecting, which had even affected innkeepers.

Already, in 1695, representations had been made to the judiciary, pointing out that the vast number of silver drinking vessels in taverns had been the cause of many crimes of violence, and requesting that steps should be taken to discourage the use of plate in this manner.

An Act was accordingly passed, forbidding innkeepers to expose any plate apart from spoons, though any who sold their silver tankards, under the pressure of this statute, are less likely to have surrendered them to the Mint for conversion into coin, than to silversmiths, who sold them to someone else.

The measures of government having failed of their purpose, they decided upon a direct onslaught on the silversmiths. In 1696 another Act was passed, with effect from 27th March 1697, compulsorily raising the standard of wrought plate to what is generally known as the 'Britannia' standard.

Plate of the new quality had to contain $11\frac{1}{2}$ ounces of pure silver in every troy pound of 12 ounces, as against the $11\frac{1}{10}$ ounces of the sterling standard, so that it became impossible for silversmiths to make use of the coinage as a raw material.

In Fig. 67 is shown a typical set of hall-marks for the year 1696, and in Fig. 68 another set for 1697.

Fig. 67. Set of hall-marks for 1696

Fig. 68. Set of hall-marks for 1697

The London Assay Office was ordered to use a new series of dies to distinguish the new quality from the old, so that a lion's head erased was substituted for the crowned lion's face, and a figure of Britannia took the place of the lion passant which had indicated the sterling standard.

At the same time, silversmiths were obliged to enter new personal marks at Goldsmiths' Hall, and whereas these had previously consisted for the most part of initials, they were now formed of the first two letters of the surname. The mark shown in Fig. 68, for example, is that of Nathaniel Locke.

Judging from the large quantity of plate produced while the Act remained in force, it would seem to have been of little value, and was finally repealed in 1719, with effect from 1st June 1720, when the Britannia standard ceased to be obligatory and became optional. Thereafter, there was a general return to the sterling standard, though metal of the higher quality was, and still is, used occasionally.

What all this amounts to, from the point of view of the student or collector, is that silver drinking vessels assayed between March 1697 and June 1720 will all be found to bear the marks appropriate to the Britannia standard, and contain a higher proportion of silver.

It is sometimes claimed that the different composition of the alloy had an effect on styles of working, the increased softness of the purer metal obliging plateworkers to adopt a more simple manner, but the case has been very much overstated.

The tankard illustrated in Plate 16a, with its boldly embossed gadroons and cabled girdle, was made during the currency of the Britannia standard, and a great deal of other plate, during the entire reign of Queen Anne, and the early part of the reign of George I, was of an equally decorative character, so it is clear that, even if silversmiths encountered some technical difficulty, they were able to surmount it without much trouble.

It is evident, of course, that the Act of 1696 must have caused an increase in the price of wrought plate, and it is quite possible that it was this fact which was responsible for the popularity of silver mugs in the late 17th and early 18th centuries. Most of them were of pint size or less, and none of them had lids, and they were therefore very much cheaper than the usual quart tankards. At all events, their manufacture began to increase enormously at the period in question.

For some years, the small bulbous mug or can with cylindrical neck, probably introduced during the reign of Charles II, remained fairly popular, but it must have been an inconvenient vessel for drinking, owing to the necessity, arising from the shape, of tilting it up until it was nearly inverted in order to empty it. It was not long, therefore, before the body was somewhat modified; in one version, the lower bulge was very much reduced in diameter, and in the other, it was merged into the upper part in a fluent curve. Examples are shown in Fig. 69 and 70.

A reform was also long overdue in the design of the handle, and in the last years of the 17th century, this feature began to assume the appearance of a miniature tankard handle, with a thumb-rest taking the place of the lid hinge of the larger vessel.

At the same time, the analogy with the parent vessel was pursued even further, and the bodies of mugs took the same slightly tapering, cylindrical form, sometimes with a narrow encircling band applied a short distance below the rim. An example displaying these various characteristics is illustrated in Fig. 71.

The two mugs shown in Figs. 70 and 71 are very important

15. Charles II Newcastle tankard of composite type. *Height: 7″*
(Victoria and Albert Museum)

16a. William III gadrooned tankard. *Height:* $6\frac{7}{8}''$
(*Victoria and Albert Museum*)

16b. Charles II two-handled cup with acanthus-leaf decoration. *Height:* $7\frac{1}{8}''$
(*Victoria and Albert Museum*)

Fig. 69. Late 17th-century mug

Fig. 70. Late 17th-century mug

Fig. 71. Cylindrical mug, late 17th century

types in the evolution of these vessels, and formed the prototypes for the great majority of mugs produced throughout the period covered by this book.

There is little to be said of mugs made of base materials mounted in silver in the late 17th century, but it seems that a fairly strong vogue commenced for mounting leather blackjacks with silver rims and sometimes foot-rings, and very often with an escutcheon on the front of the body.

These were presumably the drinking vessels of the less well-to-do, though it would appear that they were often regarded with a certain affection by their owners. This is evident from the fact that some of them were not only mounted externally, but also completely lined with silver, a process that involved the use of only slightly less precious metal than the manufacture of a silver mug or even a tankard.

Fig. 72. Silver-mounted blackjack, 17th century

An example of a silver-mounted blackjack is shown in Fig. 72, and although the contrast between the white silver and the dark jacked leather is effective enough, these vessels, in spite of their antiquarian interest, are mostly quite devoid of artistic refinement.

TWO-HANDLED CUPS

The tall standing cup, as mentioned earlier in this chapter, went into an almost fatal decline in the second half of the 17th century. It was too fine a conception to disappear altogether, but it is clear that the subjects of Charles II and his successors felt in need of a change.

This was supplied by large two-handled cups, which were obviously as widely distributed among well-to-do private individuals as among wealthy official bodies such as Livery Companies. The prototypes had already appeared before the Restoration, but various modifications, both in form and decoration, distinguish these from the later specimens which we are about to consider.

The type with ogee-shaped body tended to become wider in relation to its height, and displayed variations in handles, covers, and feet.

Handles may be dealt with quite briefly. They were either of the terminal-figure variety which we have already encountered, or consisted of simple scrolls as in Fig. 73.

Fig. 73. Scroll handle of two-handled cup, late 17th century

Covers were of two main kinds which differed in basic principle, and either fitted over the outside of the lip, or rested on top of it. The second species, which was the more common, was provided with an internal vertical flange to retain it in position, and the first was often equipped with a finial with spreading, flat top which served as a foot when the cover was inverted. This detail may have derived from a common type of Elizabethan communion cup, whose cover was designed to form a paten when inverted in the same manner.

More often than not, these cups rested upon separately made foot-rings which were soldered to the bodies, but sometimes a foot was formed by the downward extension of the base itself.

These various features may be seen in the two-handled cups with ogee bodies shown in Figs. 74 and 75. The type ceased to be fashionable before the end of the 17th century.

Fig. 74. Charles II two-handled cup with normal cover

Fig. 75. Charles II two-handled cup with cap-cover

In Plate 16b is illustrated the other contemporary species with straight sides widening somewhat towards the rim, which was usually everted. Cups of this kind were far more numerous than those considered above, and the design was more important as the prototype of others that were to come later. They were made in a large range of sizes, and were often unaccompanied by covers.

We have already seen a pre-Restoration example in Plate 13a, but those made after 1660, though basically of the same simple shape, were more graceful in outline, having a more rounded base, and a narrower foot-ring which served to emphasize the greater curvature.

Some of the smaller or cheaper varieties had no foot at all, the base of the body resting flat on the table, as in Fig. 76.

Fig. 76. Two-handled cup without foot

Several kinds of decoration were used, one of the most pleasing, and certainly the most popular, consisting of a circuit of alternate acanthus and other leaves round the lower part of the body, as on many tankards of the same period. This ornament may be seen in the Plate.

When covers occurred, they were mostly of simple form with very low, flattened domes. If the body of the vessel was plain, the cover was generally plain also, but if embossed or other decoration appeared round the base, it was usually repeated on the central portion of the cover.

Finials consisted for the most part of solid silver knobs, or of leafage arranged in a hollow spherical cluster as in the illustration. They never rose to any considerable height.

The proportions of these covered two-handled cups were admirable, and the balance between plain and decorated surfaces so nice that each enhanced the other. They were distinguished by a simple grace and dignity which were lacking from the more elaborate later members of the same large family.

These cups were mostly from about 6 to 8 inches high to the top of the finial, but were very occasionally larger. A specimen at Magdalene College, Cambridge, made in 1669, is over a foot high. The base of the vessel is embellished with simple cut-card work, the rest of the body being left plain.

The handles are somewhat unusual, but may be readily assigned to their proper period when they are recognized as a hybrid between the formal scrolled type, and the anthropomorphic variety embodying a bare-breasted female torso. There is no vestige of human form anywhere but on the topmost curve of each handle, where a crowned king's head sprouts forth in the same manner as the commoner classical female head. Another rare feature is the finial, which consists of a standing bird instead of the usual knob, but the general form and proportions of the vessel enable it to be identified as belonging to the second half of the 17th century.

Once the appearance of the main types is mastered, there is usually little difficulty in identifying slightly eccentric examples of the same period.

Many standing cups of earlier times have lost their covers, but large numbers of two-handled cups of the late 17th century were undoubtedly made without them. Like those of the pre-Restoration period, these also are generally called 'porringers' and with no more justification.

A portrait by Benedetto Gennari in the collection of Mr. H. J. Ralph Bankes, of Elizabeth Felton as Cleopatra, shows the lady in the act of putting a pearl into an acanthus-decorated silver two-handled cup of the type under discussion. The portrait was painted in the reign of Charles II, and may be presumed to pay some regard to contemporary usage in connection with drinking vessels.

As it has never been suggested that Cleopatra stirred a pearl into her porridge, we may safely assume that the cup depicted must have been of a type which was recognized at the period as a normal and reasonable drinking vessel, rather than a utensil whose primary purpose was to contain solid food.

The use of the word 'porringer' in this connection is therefore demonstrably invalid, for if the artist had been at fault in the matter, he would merely have succeeded in making a fool of himself and his client.

A vessel which is probably an actual silver porringer of the period is shown in Plate 17a.

It was in the reign of Charles II that the dining-room first became widely fashionable as a separate entity, and in such surroundings glasses were used for drinking wine and strong ale in the course of formal meals. Silver two-handled cups appear to have taken the place of standing cups for drinking on other occasions, either to assuage thirst or for pleasure.

Apart from the circuit of lightly embossed acanthus leaves, two-handled cups of the reigns of Charles II and James II were decorated also with the other types of ornament already discussed in the section on tankards, but one rare kind of treatment was almost confined to cups of cylindrical form in order to overcome technical difficulties. This was the pierced and chased outer sleeve of the kind used on the standing cup presented by Samuel Pepys to the Clothworkers' Company.

An example is shown in Plate 17b. The body of the piece was gilt, and the outer casing was in white silver. If this arrangement had been reversed, it would have been difficult to keep the underlying surface free from tarnish. The effect is one of great richness of a rather barbaric kind, which serves to disguise the lack of inspiration in the general form.

It seems possible that these cylindrical cups, which may all be identified by the same characteristic details, may have owed something to the tankards of Scandinavian type mentioned earlier in this chapter. They were of the same shape and proportions, and were usually mounted on ball, or claw-and-ball feet, which are reminiscent of the similar feet of pomegranate form found on most of the tankards in question.

Handles were of the usual types prevalent at the period, though those of scrolled form were mostly more elaborate than those which appeared on other cups, to render them harmonious with the more richly decorated bodies.

Covers were of the familiar low-domed variety, and the finials generally consisted either of clustered foliage, as in the example shown, or turned knobs.

Very rarely, the pierced casing is found on cups of the more usual curved shape. A Charles II example was presented to Colerne church, Wiltshire, a century after it was made, together with a salver decorated in the same manner. The latter is inscribed: 'This Salver and Cup belonging was given for the use of the Sacrament . . .' The terms employed and the intention of the gift provide even further evidence of the unsuitability of the word 'porringer' when applied to vessels of this kind.

In the last decade of the 17th century, two-handled cups began to be ornamented in the various ways already discussed in relation to tankards of the same part of the century, the most important being the application of cut-card work round the bases of the bodies and the covers, or alternate fluting and gadrooning, either spiralled or vertical.

The latter style became especially popular in the reign of Queen Anne, and will therefore be discussed in the next chapter.

Fig. 77. Elaborated cut-card work, late 17th century

Cut-card work tended to be more elaborate than that which immediately followed the Restoration, and was sometimes in several diminishing layers, or with the centre of the leaf-form marked by a gadroon, or an applied beaded rib as in Fig. 77, while the leaf itself was often of more ambitious shape than formerly.

The beaded rib was liable to occur also on the handles, and, as in the case of late 17th-century mugs, these handles were frequently hollow, and wrought from two pieces of sheet silver: a method which enabled them to be bolder and stouter in appearance than those cast in the solid, without any extra expenditure of precious metal (Fig. 78).

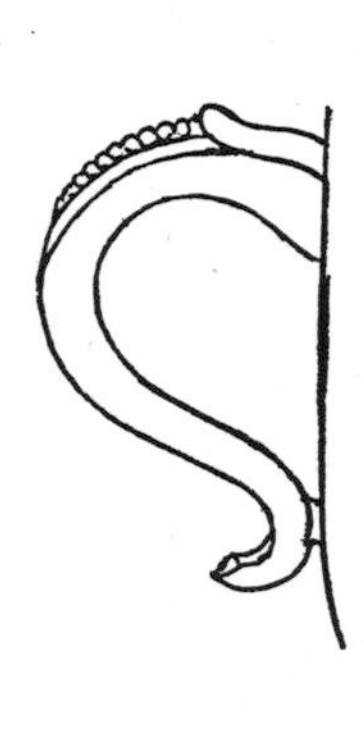

Fig. 78. Beaded wrought handle

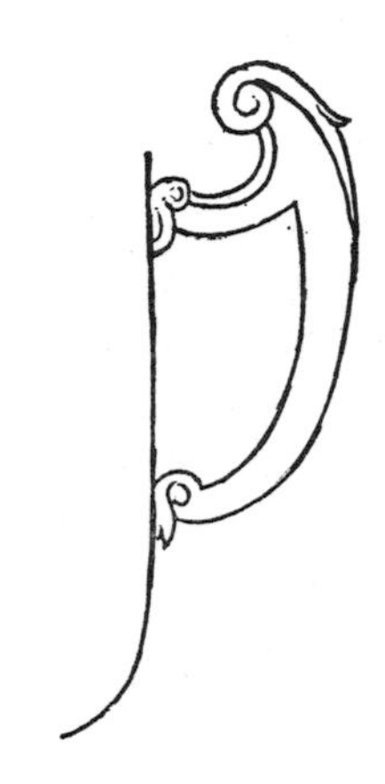

Fig. 79. Harp-shaped handle

The Huguenots were especially partial to handles constructed in this manner, but in the last years of the century they began to use an entirely novel form shaped somewhat like a harp, as in Fig. 79. It occurred in France at the same time.

In addition to these devices, covers and foot-rings were very often gadrooned round the edges.

Two-handled cups of the kind described above occur more often with the hall-marks associated with the Britannia standard, but apart from those with harp-shaped handles, they made their first appearance soon after the accession of William and Mary.

Some very fine examples of these cups were produced in Scotland at the same period, but as they bear a general stylistic resemblance to those made in England, there would be little point in discussing them in detail. Mention must be made, however, of a distinct national type which first received the attention of the silversmiths in the second half of the 17th century. This was the Quaich, a name which is a corrupt version of the Gaelic *cuach*—a cup.

Originally, this vessel was a kind of mazer, being carved out of solid wood with a shallow, wide bowl, and two, or occasionally three handles or lugs projecting horizontally from the rim, with a short downward extension at the ends.

By the middle of the century they were being built up from small vertical staves, very ingeniously fitted together, and, as in the case of mazers, were often mounted in silver, sometimes with a silver boss or print in the centre of the bowl, or even with the whole of the internal base overlaid with silver.

They seem to have been fashioned entirely in silver from about the time of the Restoration, and these silver specimens often bear a tribute to their more humble predecessors in the shape of engraved vertical lines, suggesting the coopered construction of the wooden quaichs.

An example is shown in Fig. 80. These vessels varied in diameter from about 2 to 8½ inches, but it is unlikely that even the large ones were often used for anything but spirits, the greater capacity probably implying that they were meant to be passed round among the company; a proceeding which would be facilitated by the presence of more than one handle.

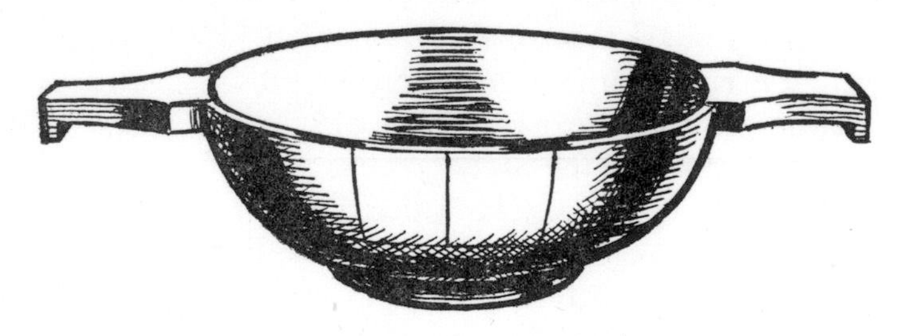

Fig. 80. Scottish silver quaich

CHAPTER FIVE

QUEEN ANNE AND EARLY GEORGIAN 1700–1760

STANDING CUPS

VERY FEW standing cups were made in the early 18th century, as their purpose was increasingly fulfilled by vessels of another kind, but it will be instructive to consider one of these rare examples.

The Pewterers' Company of London have a fine example of 1705, which is distinguished by the dignity and restraint which were characteristic of the best productions of the Queen Anne period in all branches of artistic craftsmanship. It is illustrated in Plate 18a.

The whole is conceived with the utmost thoughtfulness in the matter of decoration, the effect being produced by varying the gadroon-theme from one part to another. Basically, the form is not greatly different from that of a comparable vessel of the Charles II period, comprising a low domed foot, a bold inverted baluster stem, and a round-funnel bowl with a narrow moulding a short distance below the rim, but the decoration shows the spirit of a new age, in which feeling was combined with well-regulated conscious thought.

The low-relief, radial gadroons on the foot are closely spaced. Those on the baluster are wider apart, to prepare the eye of the observer for further developments on its upward journey. The gadroon-principle reaches its climax on the bowl, the base of which rests in a calix of widely-spaced gadroon-like ribs, on slightly wider cut-card shapes of similar form. These ribs recall the parallel feature on the 16th-century standing cup already seen in Fig. 26, and much the same thing occurred on Scottish thistle-cups.

TANKARDS

If silver vessels were no longer fashionable for drinking wine on formal occasions, the demand for tankards increased, despite the higher cost resulting from the introduction of the Britannia standard.

The changed proportions, already noted in connection with tankards made before the accession of Queen Anne in 1702, continued, and although some of these narrower vessels were liable, for a time, to be embellished with fluting and gadrooning, there is no doubt that the majority were plain of surface: a tendency that was to persist throughout the 18th century, while other contemporary silver objects were decorated in the various ways dictated by prevailing vogues.

Apart from gadrooning, all-over or partial fluting was occasionally used by itself, but the surface of a tankard treated in this manner presents such a fussy appearance, quite out of keeping with the robust and rather coarse nature of the contents, that it no doubt occurred to contemporary purchasers that there was little point in paying extra for the labour involved, when the chief result was the spoiling of an otherwise worthy vessel.

This form of treatment, which seems to have been employed mainly by Huguenot silversmiths and their copyists, was successful in providing surface interest on elegant objects such as two-handled cups, or large vessels like punchbowls and monteiths; but the rarity of tankards decorated in the same manner suggests that it was greeted with little enthusiasm by those addicted to beer-drinking, which included almost the entire population: the rich when they wanted it, the poor when they could get it.

Quite early in the 18th century, the pointed projections

disappeared from the front of the lid-flange, which returned to the plain circular shape of the time of James I, and at the same time, a low dome became practically universal on the lid itself.

This dome continued, with some variation in height and profile, throughout the period covered by this book, and remained so generally acceptable that another type of lid, introduced in the late 18th century, never managed entirely to supersede it. This will be discussed in the next chapter.

The various popular kinds of cast thumb-piece, used between the Restoration and the end of the 17th century, became largely obsolete after 1700, their place being taken chiefly by one of simple form, which became the normal type until the second half of the century: a piece of standardization which suggests a high level of production to suit a greatly expanded demand. It had made its first appearance in the late 17th century, but was exceedingly rare, and in no way typical of the period. It is commonly described as a 'scrolled' or 'volute' thumb-piece, and may be seen in Fig. 81.

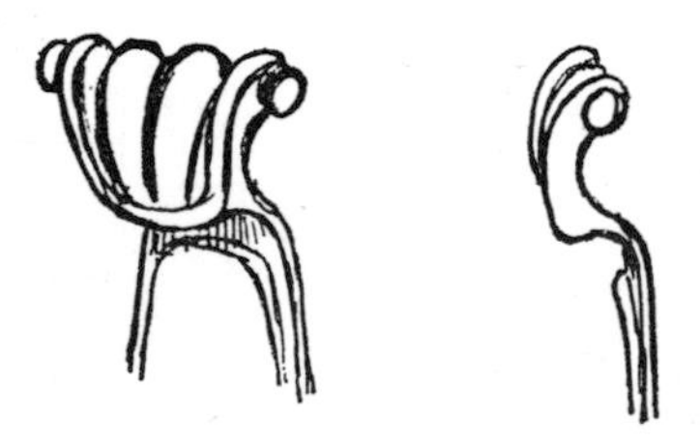

Fig. 81. Scrolled thumb-piece, early 18th century

At the same time, the cast lion thumb-piece became even more prevalent than it had been in the reign of Charles II, though its posture was sometimes altered by the different shape of the lid, which often obliged it to couch at an angle instead of horizontally. For practical purposes, it may be said that its use did not extend beyond the reign of Queen Anne, who died in 1714.

Another 17th-century feature which became common instead of rare was the thin horizontal moulding encircling the body. This occupied the usual position between the centre and just above the base, and until the reign of George III few tankards were made without this moulding, though it appears to have become temporarily less popular for a short while in the reign of George I.

It was functional as well as decorative, for it not only made the body more rigid, but also took the shock of accidental knocks which might otherwise have dented the wall of the vessel.

The embellishment of silver objects of various kinds with cut-card work was pursued with especial vigour in the first decade of the 18th century, and some tankards were treated in the same way, though their number was small in comparison with plain ones.

The decoration was mostly confined to the areas surrounding the two points where the handle was soldered to the body, but occurred occasionally in other places including the handle itself. The patterns achieved their effect either by their external line, or a combination of this with more or less elaborate piercing. Examples may be seen in Fig. 82.

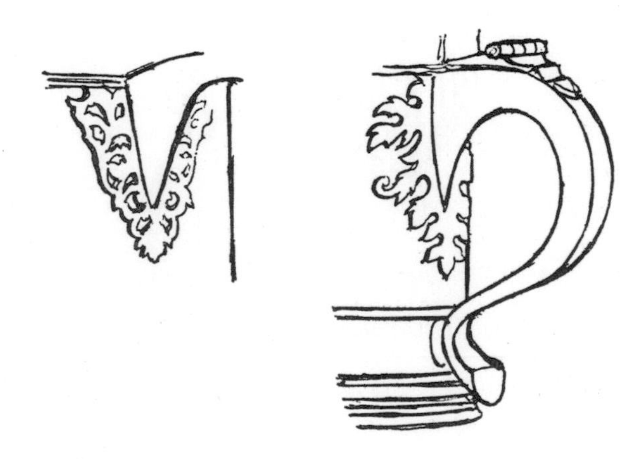

Fig. 82. Queen Anne cut-card work

During the first quarter of the 18th century a species of domestic tankard sometimes occurred with a detachable lid, which was removed by withdrawing the hinge-pin. This was attached to the handle by means of a thin silver chain to prevent its loss.

The reason for this curious feature is not clear, and the common assumption that its purpose was to enable the tankard to be temporarily converted into a mug is somewhat discounted by the occasional presence of the same detail on contemporary coffee-pots and chocolate-pots. As the removal of the lid of such a vessel would merely convert it into something which allowed all the heat to escape, we may probably assume that the feature in question was designed to facilitate cleaning. Whatever its *raison d'être*, it was never widely used, and almost entirely disappeared within a few years.

The cylindrical form of tankard body continued to be the most prevalent throughout the first half of the 18th century, often with a certain convexity of outline particularly in the first two decades, but another shape was introduced in the reign of Queen Anne, and became increasingly popular as the century advanced.

This had something of the appearance of an architectural baluster, as in Fig. 83, and for this reason these tankards are generally described as 'baluster-shaped'.

Fig. 83. Baluster-shaped tankard, early 18th century

More often than not, the body was encircled by the same sort of narrow moulding as was found on many cylindrical tankards, and as it was normally applied to the most protuberant part, was even more desirable as a protection against blows. This moulding became less common after the middle of the century.

The design may have had its beginnings in the late 17th century, when a few tankards, some made by Huguenot silversmiths, appeared with straight sides curving suddenly inward at the base just above the foot-ring, but as tankards of this kind were never anything but extremely rare, it seems more likely that the inspiration was provided by certain silver mugs of the type already seen in Fig. 70, which had the fully-developed baluster form.

This inspiration was no doubt fortified by the introduction of baluster-shaped coffee- and chocolate-pots early in the reign of Queen Anne, and as these were affected by the upper levels of society, they might be expected to have exerted some degree of stylistic pressure on other contemporary vessels of suitable shape.

The baluster was an extremely popular shape at the period, and was found, not only in architecture where it originated (Fig. 84), but also on the handles of such things as warming-pans and silver saucepans.

Fig. 84. Architectural baluster

It was evidently considered that the curvaceous appearance of the baluster-shaped bodies could be fittingly accompanied by more complex ancillary parts, and although some of them had handles of the normal kind, many were provided with double-scroll handles of the type found on tankards of the 17th-century Scandinavian form mentioned in the last chapter.

Baluster tankards were somewhat rare until the second quarter

17a. Charles II porringer. *Width:* $6\frac{7}{8}''$

(*Victoria and Albert Museum*)

17b. Two-handled cup with pierced casing. *Height:* 7″

(*British Museum*)

18a. Standing cup of the Pewterers' Company, 1705. *Height: 22½″* *(by courtesy of the Goldsmiths' Company)*

18b. Baluster-shaped tankard, mid-18th century. *Height: 6¼″* *(Victoria and Albert Museum)*

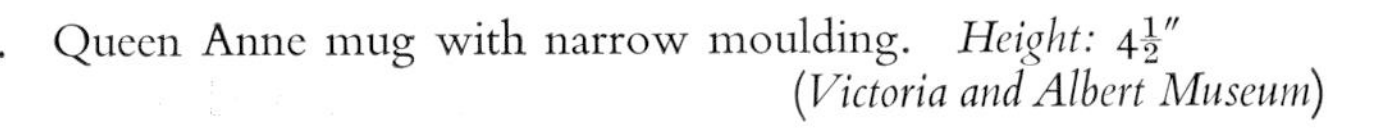

19a. Queen Anne mug with narrow moulding. *Height:* $4\frac{1}{2}''$
(*Victoria and Albert Museum*)

19b. Baluster-shaped mug, mid-18th century. *Height:* 5″
(*Victoria and Albert Museum*)

20. Two-handled cup, 1705. *Height:* $4\frac{1}{2}$″

(*Victoria and Albert Museum*)

of the century, but throughout the reign of George II were made in comparatively large numbers.

By 1750 they were becoming narrower in the body, with a more concave profile in the upper part, and the dome of the lid tended to increase in height. At the same period, thumb-pieces were more often of simple or elaborate open-work types suggestive of a chair-back (Plate 18b), though for many years there seems to have been a convention that contemporary cylindrical tankards should retain the older form of solid, voluted thumb-piece.

It is difficult to determine which of the two kinds of tankard was more popular in the middle decades of the century, as both types have survived in comparatively large numbers, but it is probable, in the author's opinion, that the cylindrical form was somewhat more prevalent until about 1750.

In the late 17th century, it had been the practice to strike the hall-marks across the top of the lid near the thumb-piece, but from 1700 onwards, they were generally applied on the inside of the dome.

This change in position is often advantageous, for it frequently happens that the marks on the body are not only struck at an angle, which makes them difficult to decipher even when they are in good condition, but their situation exposes them to so much wear that they are often almost or completely illegible. As a full set of the same marks is repeated on the inside of the lid, where they are subject to practically no wear at all, the quality, the date and place of assay, and the identity of the maker may usually be determined without difficulty.

The lids of tankards made in Exeter in the first half of the 18th century are often marked, not inside the dome, but round the flange which fits inside the rim of the vessel when the lid is closed.

It was mentioned in the last chapter that, probably owing to the increase in the price of wrought plate following the establishment of the Britannia standard, mugs began to proliferate at the turn of the century, and their popularity increased with the passage of time, no doubt involving sections of society which had previously been unable to afford silver drinking vessels.

The earliest 18th-century type was of the miniature tankard form which appeared shortly before 1700, and many Queen Anne specimens had a thin horizontal moulding encircling the body just below the lip, as in Plate 19a.

Stylistic evolution is commonly quite independent of the reigns of various monarchs, but according to the author's observation, mugs displaying the feature referred to seem to have been practically confined to the reign of Queen Anne, and it is therefore an important factor in identification.

An alternative, giving something of the same effect, was provided by a narrow encircling projection embossed from the inside, and usually contained between chased lines. This continued for some time into the reign of George I, possibly because it involved the use of no extra silver.

Other mugs made at the same time were quite plain, but all kinds might have a small oval or lozenge-shaped plate of silver soldered to the body at the lower point of attachment of the handle, as in Fig. 85.

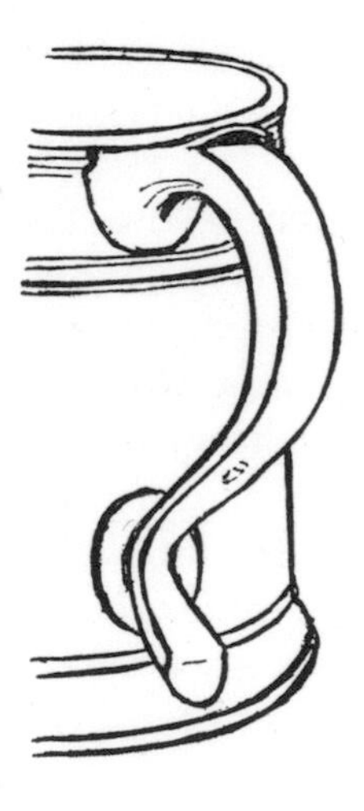

Fig. 85. Oval reinforcing plate on mug

This detail may have derived from cut-card work, of which it may be considered a humble, functional variant, but whatever its origin, it was certainly an excellent idea, for a blow on the handle of a silver mug is very liable to dent the wall of the vessel inwards, and the presence of an extra thickness of metal at the point of contact tends to reduce the likelihood of such damage.

Any collector who acquires a mug with an internal dent of the sort described should on no account attempt to hammer it out himself, as this has often resulted in a piece of silver being punched out of the body, of roughly the same size and shape as the external solder. It must be realized that the original blow has not only dented the wall, but also bent the handle to some extent, so that hammer blows on the inside are made against the springy resistance of the handle itself. A mug in this condition should be taken to a silversmith for attention.

Very occasionally, a tankard of the late 17th century is found with this same reinforcing plate between the body and the handle, but there is no doubt that it was first used at all widely on mugs in the early 18th century. Thereafter, more and more tankards displayed the same feature, until it became practically universal on both mugs and tankards.

In the first quarter of the century, a great many cylindrical mugs had a noticeable entasis or convexity of outline, but after about 1730 this either disappeared, or gave way to an actual slight concavity of profile, and at the same time, bodies tended to become taller in relation to their width, both tendencies persisting into the latter part of the century.

After 1720, a body of alternative shape enjoyed some popularity, and was characteristic of the reign of George I. It has been mentioned earlier that a rare and very small group of tankards of the late 17th century had straight sides curving suddenly inward at the base immediately above the foot-ring. This shape, which might be described as 'rounded cylindrical', was now used fairly frequently for mugs, and although it offered serious competition to the cylindrical form, it would be unsafe to assert that it was ever numerically superior. The type is shown in Fig. 86.

From the same period dates the development of a convention that while mugs with cylindrical bodies should preserve the wrought D-section handle, those with curvaceous bodies should mostly have handles of oval, circular, or polygonal section,

Fig. 87. Terminal of George I mug-handle

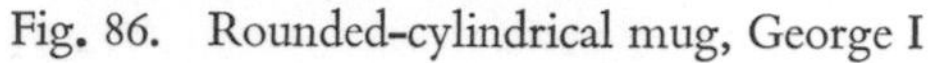

Fig. 86. Rounded-cylindrical mug, George I

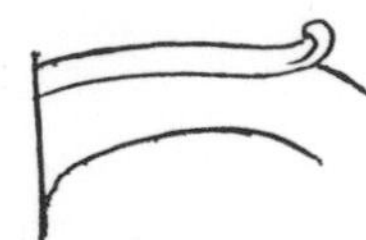

Fig. 88. Fig. 89. Fig. 90.
Thumb-rests of cast mug-handles

formed either by casting in the solid, or by casting two partly hollow halves and soldering them together vertically. Larger handles usually fall into the second category.

Those which accompanied the earlier examples of this type of mug always terminated in a simple scroll or modified ball as in Fig. 87, though the detail in question was sometimes found later at a time when more elaborate handles, and mugs of a different shape had become generally fashionable. Hybrids were always liable to occur, especially when styles overlapped, so that older-type mugs are sometimes found with newer-type handles, and *vice versa.*

Accompanying thumb-rests were of three main kinds: a tongue-like process ending in a slight upward scroll (Fig. 88), a conventionalized leaf with ribs or undulations (Fig. 89), or a simple spur rising from the top of the handle (Fig. 90). The ribbed leafage was a popular motif, and occurred on other kinds of silverware apart from mugs. It persisted far into the second half of the 18th century, and was again used extensively during the Regency, when lack of invention often induced silversmiths to resuscitate outmoded styles.

In about 1730, the bodies of fashionable mugs began to change from the rounded-cylindrical to a true baluster shape, and handles were thereafter generally of double-scroll form, terminating in a scroll and spur as in Plate 19b.

These baluster mugs, with single or double-scroll handles, have survived in large numbers, and it is clear that the middle decades of the 18th century saw a considerable increase in the demand for lidless beer vessels.

A great many, known at the time as 'cans', were of half pint size; so many, in fact, that some collectors seem to have formed the opinion that these smaller mugs were used primarily as tea-cups. The author is not aware of any reliable evidence to support this notion, and it seems against all reason.

A few silver tea-cups, mostly without handles, like their counterparts in porcelain, were indeed made in the late 17th and early 18th centuries, no doubt as part of the prevailing tendency to spread the use of plate over an ever-widening field, but it is very evident why they never became popular. Anyone who has attempted to drink a hot liquid from a silver mug will know, not only that the handle remains painfully hot for some time, but that the heat of the rim against the lips is so unbearable, that the contents cannot be drunk until they are lukewarm.

In these circumstances, it seems evident that silver half-pint mugs were simply used for cold drinks such as milk, or for beer by those who did not feel disposed to drink a pint, though there was naturally nothing to prevent their being replenished if the drinker underwent a change of heart.

A very uncommon type of silver mug of the reign of George II may be mentioned, as, although it was rare in any material at the period with which we are concerned, in the 19th century it occurred frequently in pewter, with a later and less graceful form of handle.

It had a cylindrical body and an everted lip without the usual moulding, while the base was formed after the manner of a shallow, footed cup as in Fig. 91. An example once seen by the

Fig. 91. George II mug with cast body

author in a London auction-room was unusually heavy, and appeared to have been cast and turned, but it was fully marked and seemed perfectly authentic. Mugs of this kind are unlikely to be encountered.

TWO-HANDLED CUPS

Two-handled cups of the early 18th century may be divided into two classes, both of which are easily identifiable—those with or without covers, of fairly simple appearance, designed to serve a functional domestic purpose, and those of a more monumental character, equipped with covers and more expensively produced, whose main purpose was decorative, but which might be used as loving cups on ceremonial occasions.

Entirely typical of the first category is the cup shown in

Plate 20. It is of the same general shape as the comparable vessel of the Charles II period, but is seldom found with a foot-ring, the cup resting upon the base of the receptacle itself.

The decoration, consisting of a basal circuit of vertical or spiral gadroons and flutes, with a cabled girdle higher up the body, has already been noticed as occurring on certain tankards of the turn of the century, but in the reign of Queen Anne it became exceedingly popular, and nearly all simple, functional two-handled cups of the first quarter of the century were embellished in this manner.

Scottish examples were very often quite plain, but the top of each handle sometimes bore a small knob, as in Fig. 92, to provide an extra purchase for the thumb.

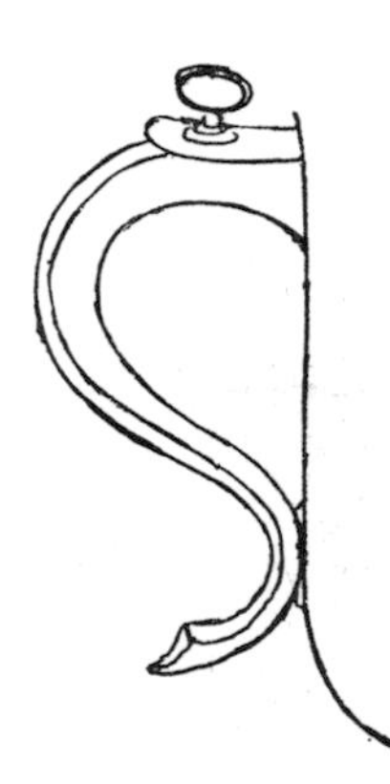

Fig. 92. Handle of Scottish two-handled cup

The incidence of these vessels began to decline steeply in the second half of the century, and the comparatively few that were produced displayed a degeneracy of proportion which makes them compare very unfavourably with their prototypes. They lost the pleasing squat appearance of earlier specimens, and became disagreeably narrow in relation to their height.

The other class of two-handled cup is represented by vessels of greater artistic merit and more important aspect, though one sometimes feels that in acquiring these qualities a certain amount of sincerity has been sacrificed. Some of the finest examples were produced by immigrant Huguenots, and native craftsmen who followed their mode of working.

Unlike a tankard, a two-handled cup is symmetrical, and capable of greater elaboration of form than a beer vessel, and it is evident that these facts were appreciated by the 'necessitous strangers', as they were described in a petition to the Goldsmiths' Company by certain English silversmiths who wished a curb to be placed on their activities.

Even before 1700 an occasional example was made with an incipient stem between the foot-ring and the base of the bowl, and in the early 18th century, this feature became an almost universal characteristic of the more important type of two-handled cup (Fig. 93). The stem became higher with the passage of time.

Fig. 93. Two-handled cup with short stem

Early in the century, the harp-shaped handles mentioned in the last chapter were much resorted to by the Huguenots, but barely survived into the reign of George I as a fashionable feature. In Ireland, they persisted for very much longer, possibly on account of an association of ideas which linked them with the Irish harp.

Other handles were of the normal scrolled variety already mentioned in connection with mugs of the period, and followed the same line of development. Earlier ones were of S-form, and terminated in a ball-like process, while those made after about 1730 tended to be of double-scroll form, ending in a scroll and spur or two opposed scrolls. Very often, the handles of mugs and two-handled cups were completely identical, and were capped with the same kind of leafage, as may be seen from Plate 21, which shows a cup of the early George II period.

This illustration serves to emphasize various significant factors in identification when compared with Fig. 93. The two most noticeable changes in proportion are in the increased height of the stem and the dome of the cover.

The second detail evolved in much the same way as the lid domes of tankards, and the handles are precisely similar to those of many contemporary mugs, but the decoration is of a kind never found on vessels of the humbler sort.

In essence, it is a variety of cut-card work, but produced by a technique far removed from that employed earlier, when elaboration was achieved by applying one layer of cut sheet-silver over another. In the example shown, the richness of the surface is due to stamping the metal with dies; a method which, while less dependent on hand-craftsmanship, undoubtedly resulted in a higher degree of sophistication.

Although the specimen illustrated in the Plate dates from the mid-1730s, we can already perceive the emergence of the ancestral origins of most of the sports trophies made from the 19th century to the present day.

One of the greatest craftsmen of the period was a second-generation Huguenot named Paul de Lamerie, and although it is only fair to say that he was no greater than an English silversmith named Kandler, he has been mentioned because his work is very highly esteemed at the present day. Like most of his compatriots, he used a great deal of cast and applied decoration, which might consist of flowers, fruit, and classical masks, executed with consummate flair. Vessels treated in this manner were very costly on account of the large amount of precious metal involved in their manufacture.

Occasionally, Lamerie's adventurous spirit and high technical skill led him into errors of taste, as in the case of a cup in the possession of the Fishmongers' Company of London, the handles of which consist of over-realistic serpents apparently twining in and out of the body of the vessel, and greatly detracting from its dignity and repose.

Lamerie was one of the first silversmiths to work in the newly-evolved Rococo style, which had appeared in France in the mid-1720s. This style consisted of a kind of organized chaos, and involved the use of such elements as broken scrolls, conventionalized rock-work, shells, and sprays of flowers. An example may be seen in Fig. 94.

Fig. 94. Rococo ornament

One might suppose that this type of decoration, with its suggestion of restless movement and deliberate defiance of symmetry, would completely destroy the balance of a design, but in spite of its fortuitous appearance, it was all conceived with the utmost care, so that a violent, asymmetrical movement in one direction was always balanced by a compensating movement in the other. The result is that although the details display a lack of formal restraint, the total effect of a Rococo design is as reposeful as any other.

One valid criticism which may be levelled at Rococo is that it tended to produce an over-emphasis on decoration at the expense of form, but on the other hand, there is no doubt that its exacting nature, which demanded the most painstaking application, brought about a general improvement in the standard of silversmiths' work.

No mention was made of the style in the section on tankards and mugs, because it was almost never used in this connection; silversmiths had an innate sense of fitness which made it distasteful to them to impart a sophisticated prettiness to vessels designed for the homely beer. The vast majority of tankards and mugs embossed in the Rococo manner began life as plain vessels which were subsequently tampered with in the Victorian period.

Fig. 95. Cup with swag-bellied body

The Victorians were not only under the impression that they knew more about mediaeval architecture than mediaeval architects did, but also that they had an infallible sense of beauty; but in fact, the chief result of their beautifying activities has been a devastating reduction in the value of the articles concerned.

Students should study genuine examples of Rococo ornament to enable them to distinguish it from the Victorian version. The latter tended to display a lack of purposefulness in the scroll-work, and a disinclination to leave any part of the surface plain, so that the background to the various elements of the design is often covered with scale-work, matting, or trellis.

During the reign of George II, the general desire for novelty led to the introduction of an unfortunate swag-bellied form in the bodies of certain hollowware, the base of the vessel above the stem being in the shape of a double ogee, as in Fig. 95.

This degenerate design was even more prevalent in the reign of George III, especially for tea-pots and coffee-pots, but although some two-handled cups were made in the same manner, the more orthodox form continued coevally, and apparently remained more popular.

CHAPTER SIX

LATE GEORGIAN

1760–1830

IN THE 18th century, men of wealth and position were in the habit of making a grand tour which brought them in contact with the erstwhile classical world. They appear, in general, to have profited little from their experience, and like most other men, accumulated a convenient set of prejudices which did duty as a philosophy of life, but one British traveller to Italy in 1754 was not a man to be bored in one place, and then move on to be bored somewhere else. He went in a spirit of artistic enquiry, and as a result of his travels, was destined to bring about a revolution in design and taste.

This man was Robert Adam, who had been trained as an architect by his Scottish father. He arrived in Italy to encounter the sensation caused in archaeological circles by the classical Roman remains already discovered during the excavations at Herculaneum, and by further discoveries made at Pompeii while he was actually in the country.

He was at once fired with the idea of adapting classical objects and ornament to the contemporary idiom, and on returning to practise as an architect in London in 1758, began to put his ideas into execution with the greatest enthusiasm.

He was of the opinion that an architect, in order to achieve general consistency, should concern himself with all the details of furnishing and decoration, including the domestic plate, and actually designed plate himself for various of his clients.

Sir John Soane said of him later: 'To Mr. Adam's taste in the ornament of his buildings and furniture we stand indebted, inasmuch as manufacturers of every kind felt, as it were, the electric power of this revolution in art.'

The 'manufacturers' included, of course, the silversmithing fraternity, and ten years after Adam became established in London, the Rococo style was almost entirely superseded by the new classical style, of which he was the most important advocate.

STANDING CUPS

In the third quarter of the 18th century, the English glass-making industry was in a flourishing state despite the Glass Excise Act of 1745, and it is a great tribute to the strength of the Adam influence that a partial return was made to silver standing cups, conceived in a very fair rendering of the classical manner.

Fig. 96. Goblet of the Adam period

These silver goblets had large ovoid bowls, sometimes decorated with fluting, and simple, concave-sided stems merging smoothly into feet which might be circular, square, or polygonal. These forms were soon reproduced in the rummers of the glass-makers, and although these cheaper vessels were naturally far more numerous than their counterparts in silver, it is remarkable, in view of the fact that silver standing cups had been out of favour for a hundred years, that they were able to be repopularized at all. An example is shown in Fig. 96.

The generous capacity of these cups suggests that they were used for beer or beverage wine, and they may well have caused a decline in the number of mugs made after about 1770.

TANKARDS

Most of the tankards of the reign of George III were of the baluster-shaped variety introduced earlier in the century, but were more often narrower in the body, and with a deeper foot-ring and a higher dome to the lid, as in Fig. 97.

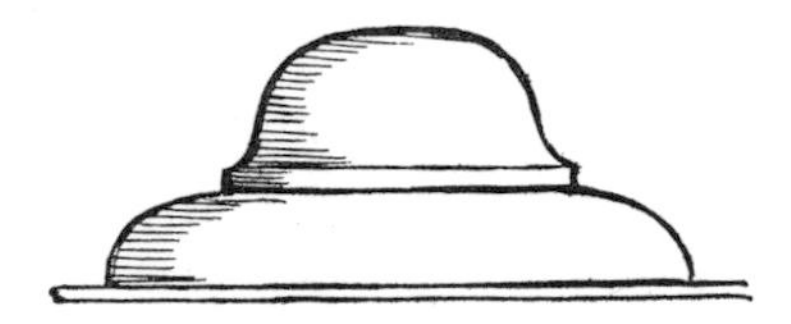

Fig. 97. Tankard-lid, late 18th century

The same change in proportion was also characteristic of contemporary cylindrical tankards, and the lids were of the same kind.

Both were the victims of a certain amount of mass-production. Most tankards of the first half of the century were raised by the hammer from a single disc of sheet-silver without any joint in the body, but it became the practice later for the body to be soldered together vertically, the seam running down the back at the point where the handle was attached. A separate disc of silver was soldered into the bottom to form a base.

Cylindrical tankards often displayed a certain concavity of profile, and in this part of the century, were encircled with a narrow horizontal moulding more frequently than those of baluster shape.

Towards the end of the century, tankards were sometimes

made of such thin silver, that it was considered desirable to increase their apparent weight and add to their stability.

This was done by loading them with lead, which was poured into the space between the edge of the foot-ring and the base of the body, and covered with a disc of copper with green baize glued to its surface. Loaded tankards seem to have been produced mostly at Birmingham and Sheffield, where assay offices had been opened in 1773.

These late tankards were fully marked on the bodies, but it became the practice to mark the lids with the sterling quality mark only.

In the last quarter of the century appeared two new kinds of tankard differing somewhat in shape, but generally related in style. The rarer of the two had a body shaped like a cask, possibly to accord with the Prussian-shaped decanters then in vogue, and was often engraved with bands and vertical lines to suggest hoops and staves. The other had a tapering cylindrical body also often engraved with lined bands, but seldom with vertical staves.

Both had the same kind of lid, handle, and hinge, which were very distinctive, and enable the types to be identified without difficulty.

The first represented, in effect, a return to the Charles I period, and was almost flat, resting on the moulding round the lip of the body, and without the customary internal flange.

The handle was usually of rectangular section, and of a shape not previously encountered. The lower part sometimes finished flush against the body instead of curving away in the usual manner.

The hinge, which can scarcely be considered an improvement on the traditional style, consisted of two arms projecting from the back of the lid, and pinned straight through the sides of the handle. All these features may be seen in Fig. 98.

Mugs were made in the same styles and in a large range of sizes, but it must be emphasized that most of the mugs and tankards in the period under discussion were of baluster shape. These were produced by many manufacturers, and although mostly well made, were within the competence of even second-rate

21. Two-handled cup with stem, 1736. *Height:* $12\frac{1}{4}''$
(*Victoria and Albert Museum*)

22. Cylindrical mug, late 18th century. *Height: 5″*
(*Victoria and Albert Museum*)

23. Two-handled cup in the Adam style. *Height:* 1 4″
(*Victoria and Albert Museum*)

24a. Regency mug. *Height:* 4″
(*Victoria and Albert Museum*)

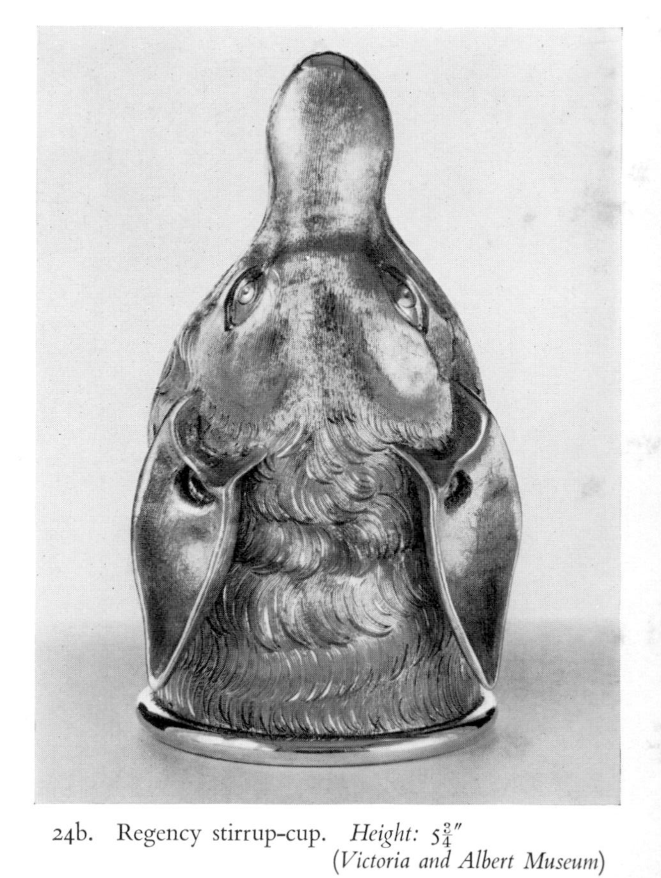

24b. Regency stirrup-cup. *Height:* $5\frac{3}{4}$″
(*Victoria and Albert Museum*)

silversmiths such as Hester Bateman, whose productions have, of recent years, attracted the attention of some collectors to an extent which is by no means justified by their merit.

Normal cylindrical mugs were also made, though they were far less numerous than those of baluster shape. They were of the same proportions as the similar tankards, and had the same deep foot-rings. An example may be seen in Plate 22.

Fig. 98. Tankard with flat lid, late 18th century

In accordance with a long-established convention, most of them had wrought handles of the usual D-section, but the thumb-rests were often different from those of earlier specimens. They still consisted of a strip of sheet silver with a curved end, soldered to the open top of the handle, where a space had been left to receive it, but instead of being almost flat or concave, as previously, were frequently in prolongation of the outer curve of the handle, as in the example shown in Plate 22.

Collectors should beware of unusually large mugs with thumb-rests of this kind, as many of them were once tankards which have lost their lids and had the hinges removed.

A few cylindrical mugs of the period were raised in one piece from plate of thin gauge, but for the most part they were seamed down the back, and had separate base-discs.

TWO-HANDLED CUPS

Two-handled cups were, if anything, more susceptible of neo-classical treatment than standing cups, especially as antiquity furnished a ready-made example which needed very little adaptation.

This was the classical urn, a form which was easily convertible into all kinds of hollowware such as tea-pots, coffee-pots, hot water jugs, sugar vases, and tea canisters, and more easily still into two-handled cups.

The usual shape was similar to that of the standing cups already discussed, but on a larger scale, and the cup was also equipped with a cover, and two graceful handles rising above the rim, and curving downward in a sweeping arc to the base of the receptacle. Others were of the usual S-shape, but generally rose high above the rim of the cup.

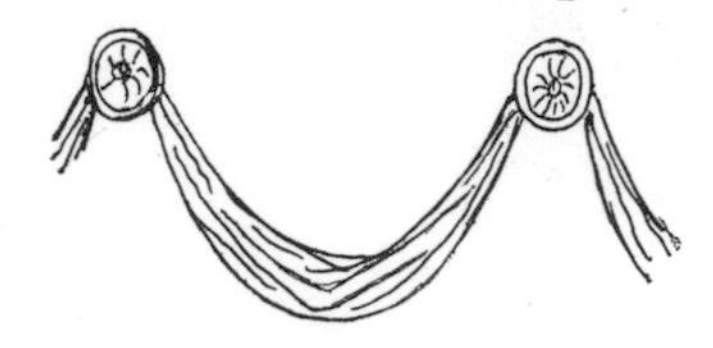

Fig. 99. Swags of cloth and husks, Adam period

Plate 23 illustrates a fine example of the Adam period, and shows a typical assortment of decoration, including stiff leafage on the foot, the base of the bowl, and the cover, a scrolling vine-trail round the rim, an applied band with classical wave-crest ornament, and between these, a variant of the motif perhaps more characteristic of the style than any other—a circuit of swags.

In the example shown, these are entirely floral in character, but they also commonly consisted of draped cloth or festoons of husks, as in Fig. 99. Acanthus leaves and medallions were also widely used.

This ornament was either cast and applied, embossed, or a mixture of both, and was sometimes eked out by beaded edges, and what is known as 'bright-cut engraving'; a kind of small-scale shallow chip-carving, which caught the light in an agreeable manner, and added to the surface interest without disguising the form.

Some of these cups, which were occasionally gilded, were of very large size, and it seems likely that they had little functional purpose at all. They could certainly be used for drinking group-toasts, and passing from hand to hand, but it is probable that they spent most of their existence adding lustre to the handsome mahogany sideboards and other pieces of furniture designed by Adam himself, or copyists such as Hepplewhite who adapted existing vernacular versions of his designs.

They were not all as ornate as the example illustrated, and a great many were entirely plain apart from bright-cut engraving, or a circuit of narrow flutes or gadroons rising up from the base, and usually repeated on the foot and the cover.

These, and others with no ornament at all, relied for their effect on the well-bred restraint and beauty of proportion which were characteristic of nearly all artistic productions of this elegant and distinguished period.

In 1784, an important change occurred in relation to hall-marking which involved the compulsory application of another mark in addition to those already in use.

This new stamp, which took the form of the sovereign's head, was required to be struck on plate to indicate that duty had been paid according to the weight of the object concerned. Forging the mark was punishable by death.

The law which imposed the new obligation came into force on

1st December 1784, and was not repealed until 1890, during which time, all wrought plate subject to marking bore the heads of successive sovereigns, though there was a certain amount of overlapping in the use of dies.

THE REGENCY STYLE

It is perhaps unnecessary to mention that the reign of George III extended to 1820, and that the Regency actually began in 1811, when the King became incapable of discharging his office through insanity. The Regency style began to appear, however, in about 1800, though the Adam influence lingered on to some extent into the early 19th century, so that the two overlapped. The new style continued up to the date at which this survey concludes.

The difference between the two styles is easier to recognize than describe. Both were classical in origin, and shared various elements of clasical ornament and design, but the later of the two was heavy rather than elegant, and was based, in fact, on a heavier and later phase of Roman art.

Functional drinking vessels of silver were tending to become less popular at the period, but those that were made were often unaffected by the grosser manifestations of Regency taste, which placed great value on massiveness, and foreshadowed the coming Victorian degeneracy.

STANDING CUPS

The silver goblets which had appeared during the Adam period continued to enjoy some popularity in the early 19th century, but soon after 1800, a type was introduced with a bowl of different shape. This was based on a heavier kind of classical urn, and had something of the appearance of a thistle, as in Fig. 100.

The gadrooned protuberance at the base of the bowl was particularly common, and some were otherwise plain, while others bore further decoration. This frequently took the form of a finely executed fruiting vine, cast separately, and

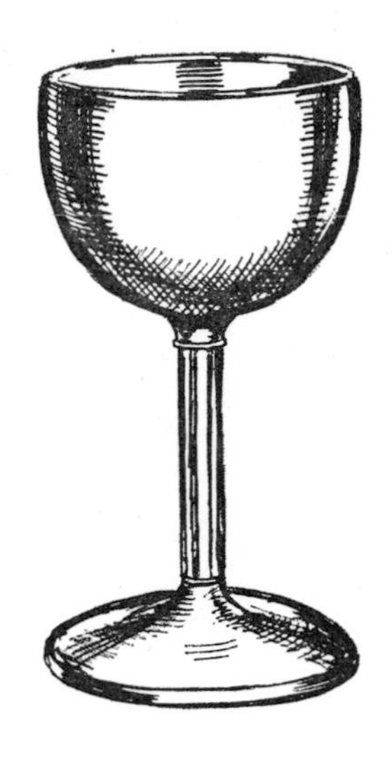

Fig. 100. Regency goblet

Fig. 101. Regency goblet of wine-glass form

applied by solder in a band round the upper part of the bowl.

Whatever the forms of decoration used, identification may be based most conveniently on the general shape of the vessel.

Another sort of small standing cup was in the form of a certain kind of contemporary drinking glass. The type is shown in Fig. 101. It seems probable that the glass came first, rather than the silver cup, but it was, in any event, of too paltry a design to be worthy of reproduction in a precious material.

Apart from functional vessels, some of which were pleasing and well proportioned, the standing-cup form was sometimes used for objects intended only for display, as in the case of the National Cup of 1824 at Windsor Castle.

This curious object owes nothing to classical sources, but is inspired by a degenerate mediaevalism. The domed cover is surmounted by a figure of St. George and the dragon, and the body, which is of a complicated shape that almost defies description, is embellished with three deeply-modelled Gothic niches, flanked by columns, containing figures of St. George, St. Patrick, and St. Andrew. The stem is cylindrical, with a flattened ball-knop, while the rim of the foot rests upon a circuit of depressed ogival Gothic arches, so that the cup is supported on the bases of the spandrels, like a claw-and-ball foot without the ball.

In spite of the high technical skill manifested in the execution of the details, this cup can hardly be considered as anything but an artistic abomination, and although such objects are fortunately rare, the one described serves as a pointer to the stylistic uncertainty which began to prevail during the late Regency.

TANKARDS

The tankards and mugs in use during the Regency are barely to be distinguished from those which were current before 1800, and it is not possible to draw attention to any conclusive identification factors in connection with most of them. Both sorts of vessel appear to have declined in popularity, and there were quite possibly almost sufficient surviving 18th-century specimens available to satisfy demands, without a great deal of additional production.

One type of mug, however, of strongly late-classical appearance, and of a kind not hitherto known in England, began to be made in the first quarter of the 19th century.

It was shaped more or less like a bucket, with a stoutly-modelled foot-ring and everted lip. Decoration varied, but was mostly beautifully designed and executed, and although it was sometimes liable to give the mug more the air of an *objet d'art* than an object of use, there can be no doubt of the aesthetic merit of such vessels, which would be a credit to any period.

An example is shown in Plate 24a. Such pieces of Regency plate emphasize the fact that silversmiths of the period could acquit themselves nobly when they were not over-ambitious, whereas more monumental productions were very liable to be distinguished chiefly by a slightly vulgar pomposity, and an impression of eminent meltability.

TWO-HANDLED CUPS

Most of the two-handled cups of the early 19th century were either sports trophies or presentation pieces whose size, importance, and monumental character gave them the status of vases rather than functional drinking vessels. The same form was also employed for many objects such as sugar-bowls, sauce-tureens, and the tops of centrepieces, but as none of these would ever have been used as drinking vessels, they are outside the scope of this book.

The handles of original Regency cups were usually of a basically different character from those of the 18th century. They sometimes rose vertically from opposite sides of the rim of the bowl,

Fig. 102. Regency cup with volute handles

then curled inwards in a volute, as in Fig. 102. A series of cups of this kind was made for the Patriotic Fund of Lloyds for presentation to senior naval officers who had been present at the Battle of Trafalgar in 1805.

Fig. 103. Regency cup with horizontal handles

Some cups had short handles which were attached horizontally near the base of the vessel, as in Fig. 103, while others had them rising vertically from the same position to about half-way up the bowl.

Cups of the latter sort were often in a modified version of the thistle shape already mentioned, but usually had a merely rudimentary stem as in Fig. 104. Some were decorated in a manner which gave them a heavy, sculptural character, being embellished with classical figure-subjects in relief, more suitable for execution in stone or bronze than in silver.

Apart from the foregoing, which were all creations of the early

19th century based on Imperial Roman originals, many others displayed the eclecticism which was beginning to manifest itself, and were passable reproductions of George II vessels of the type illustrated in Plate 21, while others were decorated with Rococo ornament, which had been out of fashion since about 1770.

Fig. 104. Regency cup of modified thistle shape

The last may sometimes be detected by the presence, among the broken Rococo scrolls, of typically Regency elements such as late classical fruiting vines and cupids, but one is unfortunately obliged, in many cases, to base identification on the hall-marks, rather than the form or decoration.

A popular oddity of the hard-drinking, hard-riding days of the Regency was the silver Stirrup-cup. These cups had first appeared sparsely in the second half of the 18th century, but they became exceedingly popular in the early 19th century, and the great majority of examples encountered will almost certainly date from this period, of which they are more typical than any other.

They were nearly all in the form of a hollow fox's mask or hound's mask, with the ears, generally attached by solder, either projecting, or more usually lying back along the head. The fur was rendered with much realism. They varied somewhat in capacity, but most of them hold about half a pint. An example of the period is illustrated in Plate 24b.

These Regency stirrup-cups were nearly all cast, and are usually rather heavy in consequence, whereas 18th-century specimens were mostly hand-wrought with much painstaking labour, and had deeper rims which were often engraved with inscriptions relating to fox-hunting or coursing. As indicated above, however, the average collector is very unlikely to come across an example made before the early 19th century.

Much of the more important plate of the Regency period was conceived by professional designers such as John Flaxman and Charles Heathcote Tatham, whose assumption of authority in matters of taste increasingly relegated the silversmith to the position of a skilled artisan who executed someone else's designs.

It is probable that the growing decline in the aesthetic merit of plate at this period may be largely attributed to this particular factor, but in any event, the heyday of English silver drinking vessels was over.

SELECTED BIBLIOGRAPHY

BRADBURY, FREDERICK. *Guide to Marks of Origin on British and Irish Silver Plate*, 8th edition. 1950.

CRIPPS, W. J. *Old English Plate*. 1878.

FINLAY, IAN. *Scottish Gold and Silver Work*. 1956.

HAYWARD, J. F. *Huguenot Silver in England, 1688–1727*. 1959.

JONES, E. ALFRED. *Old Plate of the Cambridge Colleges*. 1910.

JACKSON, SIR CHARLES J. *English Goldsmiths and Their Marks*. 1921. *An Illustrated History of English Plate*. 1911.

MOFFATT, H. C. *Old Oxford Plate*. 1906.

OMAN, C. C. *English Domestic Silver*. 1947.
English Church Plate. 1957.

WATTS, W. W. *Old English Silver*. 1924.

INDEX